T0285886

LOST
DELAWARE

LOST DELAWARE

RACHEL KIPP & DAN SHORTRIDGE

THE History PRESS

Published by The History Press
Charleston, SC
www.historypress.com

Front cover: The dairy barn at the Winterthur estate, shown here in 1925, was once home to three hundred Holstein cows. After the death of the du Pont family member who was most passionate about their care, they were sold at auction in 1969. *Delaware Public Archives.*

First published 2024

Manufactured in the United States

ISBN 9781467156424

Library of Congress Control Number: 2023949538

To Dean Hume, who taught me how to love writing and to pursue great stories.
—RK

To the late John Gates and Bill Williams,
who taught me how to document history.
—DS

CONTENTS

ACKNOWLEDGEMENTS

A book of history like this is not the sole work of the authors. It is the product of generations of journalists, historians and people like you who have documented and shared the small stories of local history. From letters to the editor to articles in church newsletters, we must preserve as many of these stories as we can.

We want to first thank the historians whose work we found exceptionally helpful, including Constance J. Cooper, George J. Frebert, Allan Girdler, Doug Gelbert, Carol Hoffecker, Ed Kee, Michael Morgan, James Diehl, W. Barksdale Maynard, John Medkeff, Michael J. Nazarewycz, Douglas Poore, John Scharf, Bradley Skelcher, Jon Springer, Bob Trapiani Jr. and Frank Zebley. Writers for the *Cape Gazette*, *Coastal Point*, *Delaware Independent*, Delaware Public Media, *Delaware State News*, *Delaware Today*, *News Journal*, University of Delaware *Review*, WHYY and other media outlets wrote much of history's first draft. Their books and articles are all listed in the bibliography.

History is made much easier to appreciate and understand through photographs and illustrations, which bring the past to life. Thanks are also due to Jen Ellingsworth and Chris Flood of the *Cape Gazette*; Jason Miller of the Delaware Department of Correction; Rony J. Baltazar-Lopez of the Delaware Department of State; Shauna McVey and Taylor Reynolds of Delaware State Parks; Leigh Rifenburg and Bill Robinson of the Delaware Historical Society; Angela Schad and Doug McQuirter of Hagley Museum and Library; and the incredible staff of the Delaware Public Archives, who go above and beyond the call of duty in assisting researchers in retrieving and reproducing photographs.

All that said, any errors or omissions contained here are our own.

A giant thanks is owed to Kate Jenkins, our liaison and all-round project steward from The History Press, whose attention to detail and attention to the calendar were invaluable and incredibly helpful during the research and writing of this book.

And the biggest thank-you of all goes to our families, who helped throughout the many logistical challenges of working jobs, raising children and writing a book, even during their own trying times. To our children, Dassi, Liam and Matty, we especially thank you for your everlasting patience, wisdom and good humor.

INTRODUCTION

Judging by this book, Delaware loses a lot of things. We've sadly waved farewell to an entire language, resorts for relaxation, hospitals for healing, bridges for crossing and lighthouses for navigation. Gone are restaurants, mansions, drive-ins and an oddball event where cannons and trebuchets launched pumpkins. Malls, retail stores and open-air markets have all disappeared. And we've even lost an entire community washed away by flooding.

But among those stories are the bright spots: the autoworkers who bought homes and started families on good union wages. The students who studied in the schools, even as state-sanctioned racism kept them separate and apart. The drugstore chain with the happy face and happier employees inside. The inventors who dreamed of those odd new aeroplanes and made them fly.

Those are the stories we hope you take away from this book. It is, above all, a chronicle of Delaware's colorful past and of its vibrant people.

Lost Delaware is also a tribute to the preservationists who work to keep the special places intact and alive, who refuse to leave to memory the sights and sounds of the past and who struggle against the odds to ensure that history is maintained for future generations. Oftentimes they fail, but it's darn sure not for lack of trying.

Choosing the stories to share in this book was the second-most difficult part; the most difficult was fitting them all in the pages of this book. We began with a much longer list, but some stories just flowed once we began researching and writing. We decided they should take up the space that they deserve. In the end, we hope you'll enjoy the seventy-one tales that we have to offer.

Rachel Kipp and Dan Shortridge
Dover, Delaware

1
AGRICULTURE

Family farmers are the core of Delaware's historic and modern agricultural industry. The state has 2,300 family farms—98 percent of the total—growing crops and raising animals. Many of the businesses once linked to agriculture, such as canning and popular large open-air markets, have long since vanished, but their stories remain.

GREENABAUM CANNERY

The second half of the 1800s saw an explosion of the mid-Atlantic canning trade. Canning coincided with the growth of the railroads—shelf-stable cans stacked in cases were easier to transport than perishable produce, as agricultural historian Ed Kee explains in his history of the regional industry, *Saving Our Harvest*. It was also cheaper to set up canneries in rural areas close to where their raw inputs were grown. In 1889, it was estimated that 41 percent of canneries in the United States were located in one region: Delaware, Maryland, Virginia and New Jersey. Delaware was home to forty-nine canneries, 3 percent of the nation's total.

One of the largest canneries during the boom era was Greenabaum Bros. of Seaford. Emanuel Greenabaum, born in Missouri in 1858, was the son of a clothing store owner in Seaford. He and his brother-in-law, Charles Van

Leer, formed the enterprise in 1886 as an oyster packer and shipper, growing into the canning business.

Heralded by the local press as "Seaford's well-known canners," Greenabaum Bros. was indisputably one of the largest canneries in Delaware and sometimes described as the biggest in the world. Throughout the 1890s, it produced 1.4 million cans of peas, peaches, pears and, of course, tomatoes. By 1897, it employed two hundred people canning peas alone. A few years later, Greenabaum was putting up 660,000 cans of peas in one week—120,000 cans in a single day. "This was the largest week's work ever done by this firm and there is not another one in the country that can pack as many peas in a week as they can," a newspaper boasted.

In 1898, Greenabaum employed three hundred workers and had six hundred on hand during tomato season. The company added on to a storage building, almost doubling its size, and installed improved canning machinery. In 1899, "the most prosperous tomato season Seaford has ever experienced," it canned ten thousand baskets of tomatoes each day, according to the scribes. The company also sold ketchup under the Sundale brand.

"If we had several more firms like the above Seaford would be on the boom," a journalist reflected.

7000 BASKETS OF TOMATOES AT GREENABAUM CANNERY, SEAFORD, DEL.

The brothers Greenabaum founded a thriving cannery in Seaford, producing canned tomatoes and peas and selling Sundale ketchup. *Delaware Public Archives.*

Yet the work was not all high wages and general prosperity. Some workers were injured, often badly. Charles O. Wilson, a Black veteran of the Great War who worked at Greenabaum, was severely burned on his arms, back and neck one day. A blower had been left open on a furnace, causing the flames to shoot out at him.

Emanuel Greenabaum died in 1924. He had been a Mason, a Seaford fire company member, a charter member of the Crescent Club and a director of First National Bank, and his son had succeeded him in the business. For the Greenabaums, canning was the road to riches and influence.

In 1938, a local paper reported that Greenabaum and other canneries in Sussex had to stay open on Sundays and at night to handle the influx of tomatoes ferried up the Nanticoke River to Seaford. But by the next decade, Greenabaum's had closed. The exact year is uncertain, but it was prior to 1948, when a fire destroyed a sheet metal warehouse along the Nanticoke at the foot of Porter Street. A newspaper reported the warehouse had been mostly empty since Greenabaum's shut down, aside from holding magazines and newspapers that local Scouts had collected.

STRAWBERRY FIELDS

For decades, strawberries reigned supreme as Delaware's queen crop—rising to succeed peaches after a disease called "peach yellows" decimated that harvest. Fields across Delaware were filled with the tiny, delicious fruit and plucked from the vine at the height of ripening. Strawberry pickers were hired from big cities, working through the night and early morning to pick the berries and put them in baskets. The berries were then loaded onto wagons, which ferried them to depots for further loading onto refrigerated railcars. Buyers camped on the streets of Selbyville to prepare for the wagons' arrival and ship them to larger cities.

In 1899, Delaware farmers grew more than 10 million quarts of berries. Sussex County was the largest strawberry producer in the nation, turning out 7 million quarts. Bridgeville shipped 1.5 million quarts each year and was the focal point of Delaware's strawberry sector. Selbyville, which picked its strawberries a little earlier in the season, was a close second.

Strawberries almost died out as a major crop by the early 1920s, when the fertile Sussex soil became less so and farmers turned to other crops. But a

In 1925, when this photograph was taken, Selbyville was one of Delaware's strawberry hubs. Fruit buyers filled the streets to get the choicest berries. *Delaware Public Archives.*

new state road running north and south the length of the state—the DuPont Highway, US 13—led to a rally, as the thoroughfare provided growers a new way to ship their strawberries. They turned from the cold cars on the tracks to "cold-packed" barrels riding in trucks up and down the highway. Farmers kept their individual cold-pack process a secret but most importantly included only good-quality berries; a single bad berry might ruin the entire barrel.

A snapshot in time gives an idea of the scope and scale of the industry. In 1935, Delaware farmers grew 4,900 acres of strawberries at 83 crates per acre—nearly 2,000 quarts' worth. Farmers received $2.10 per crate; the pickers in the field earned $0.03 to $0.05 for each quart. That year, Delaware shipped 407,000 crates or 9,768,00 quarts.

But as the population and demand for land grew, the number of farms declined, and the berry market gradually shrunk with them. Other parts of the country caught on to strawberry-selling, and Delaware farmers moved to more profitable products. By 2017, the most recent year for which federal figures are available, there were twenty-six farms growing strawberries on forty-one total acres in Delaware.

THE COWS OF WINTERTHUR

Winterthur is today known as a historic former du Pont estate and modern-day museum with vast expertise in art preservation and restoration. Its holdings and its grounds are among Delaware's most prominent and recognizable cultural features.

But Winterthur began as a private home and a working farm. Under Henry Francis du Pont's management, Winterthur focused on breeding a powerful dairy herd and boosting its milk production. H.F., as he was known, bought four Minnesota bulls and two cows for $70,000, or about $1.6 million today, to serve as the "Foundation Herd." H.F. started a breeding program with results noted in "Herd Books" and brought only the best bulls and cows together to produce offspring.

By 1926, Winterthur was home to three hundred registered Holsteins that turned out eleven thousand pounds of milk per year on average. A cow known as Winterthur Boast Ormsby Ganne broke the record for fat yield in 1933.

Pictured in 1925, the dairy barns at Winterthur once held hundreds of cows. Henry Francis du Pont's management led them to win multiple prizes. *Delaware Public Archives.*

The cows also changed the landscape at Winterthur, with a large array of barns built on Farm Hill. There were bull barns, a hospital barn and one for calves, as well as a creamery that handled ten thousand pounds of milk per day. The cows were milked twice daily, and the milk was sold to a local dairy and to Winterthur employees, bearing the motto "Milk for Better Babies from Winterthur Farms."

After Henry Francis du Pont's death in 1969, the Winterthur cows were sold at an auction. Today, goats and merino sheep live at Winterthur, in a barn near the main entrance to the storied estate.

KING STREET MARKET

As long as there have been farmers, there have been markets for their meats, fruits and vegetables. Wilmington is no different. From its earliest days, Willingtown, as it was called then, was home to two market houses for commerce and trade—one at Fourth and Shipley Streets and one at Market and Second Streets. Each received certain days of the week to be open. Butchers in particular flocked to the market stalls; indeed, a law passed in 1747 required that meat be sold in the markets and nowhere else.

Territories and schedules made the market operations complex. Historian Constance J. Cooper deftly described the confusing system that evolved by the 1860s:

> *Hucksters, who could do business every day but Saturday, used stalls under the northern eaves of the Second Street market house, the north side of Second Street between Market and King, and the north side of Fourth Street between Market and Shipley. The New Jersey farmers could sell on the south side of Second Street between Market and King, in stalls under the south eaves of the Fourth Street market house, and, on Saturdays only, on the south side of Fourth Street between Market and Shipley. Fish dealers had the west side of King between Second and Third, two stands at the King Street end of the Second Street market house, two stands at the Orange Street end of the Fourth Street market house, and twenty-two stalls under the north eaves of the Fourth Street market house….Ice cream dealers had to be under the wings of the market houses.*

Most important to note is that the two market houses were at opposite ends of King Street, with an open-air street market in between. As the market houses moved from government control to private, King Street was on the verge of becoming something entirely different and new. By the 1880s, King Street was filled with about 120 businesses—milliners, offices, industrial shops and food, of course. It was home to two butchers, bakers, candymakers, fish and fruit dealers (not the same store), general grocers and produce retailers. That didn't count the market houses, which brought a total of 86 more food sellers to King Street, including 78 butchers and 7 produce salesmen.

On the designated market days, between 200 and 300 farmers backed their wagons to the King Street curbs to sell their wares: apples, grapes, tomatoes, wildflowers, eggs, cheese and butter. One person recalled the market atmosphere from the 1890s: "Each housewife was sure she knew where the best sausage and scrapple were to be had, whose peas were the sweetest and which farmer's wife made the best cottage cheese."

A few years later, by 1900, Wilmington was home to seventy-six thousand souls, and King Street housed about 240 businesses and shops. Technology changed the markets, too, with streetcar tracks laid in 1901 that increased

Wilmington's King Street once boasted an open-air farmers' market, plus two market houses and ten food stores. *Delaware Public Archives.*

and simplified access. And other types of operations were moving in: A bottler, oyster dealer, and flour and feed dealer joined the ranks in the surrounding neighborhood. The beginning of the twentieth century was the peak of the King Street market, "a busy crowded place, full of interesting sights and smells," Cooper wrote.

But by the 1920s, the markets were losing ground to canned goods and prepared foods. The automobile gave customers more choices and altered the streetscapes. Wilmington was growing, but King Street was shrinking, with about a quarter fewer businesses than before. The two market houses closed, and food shops were replaced with other goods and services, including furniture stores. And then came the supermarkets, such as the Acme that opened on King Street in 1940. The forces of modernity proved the death knell for the King Street open-air market, which finally moved away in 1974 to a series of other locations.

A revitalization effort from city leaders led to a new farmers' market on a parking lot on Orange Street—but by 2002, only two vendors were still around. The market was eventually moved to Rodney Square, where around forty vendors today sell prepared foods, fresh produce, flowers and more, all within walking distance of downtown.

CHIPMAN SWEET POTATO HOUSE

Before poultry, there was the sweet potato. For four decades, sweet potatoes, a mainstay of the American Thanksgiving table, preceded chickens as the powerhouse of Sussex County's farming economy.

The sweet potato boom in Sussex County began around 1900, after farmers realized the area's mild climate and light, sandy soil created the perfect environment to grow what was then a profitable cash crop. The Delaware sweet potato was known for "a richness and a sweetness of flavor, which we do not find in the Carolina potato or even those grown on the rich soils of Texas," according to the 1868 Delaware State Directory. The 1924 crop was estimated to exceed one million bushels at nearly $2.75 a basket, the *Wilmington Sunday Morning Star* reported. Delaware farmers sold sweet potatoes both in-state and regionally, even offering mail delivery.

"Delaware farmers who go in for sweet potato raising are making the best 'killing' they have ever enjoyed," the *Morning Star* noted.

Sweet potato houses came about because farmers needed a place to cure their crop, which helps to sweeten the flavor, and also to store the sweet potatoes over the winter as they waited for the most profitable time to sell them. The structures had to let in air and light but also had to stay constantly and consistently warm so the sweet potatoes wouldn't freeze. The Chipman Sweet Potato House near Laurel was built in 1913 by Joseph and Ernest Chipman, with help from Alva Hudson. In addition to sweet potatoes, the Chipmans also grew Indian corn, peas, tomatoes, cucumbers, cantaloupes and strawberries.

The two-and-a-half-story sweet potato house had storage bins on the first and second floors, with several windows to let in light to help air-dry the crop. The Chipmans and other farmers used innovative techniques to keep the potatoes warm at a time when many private homes didn't have heating or insulation. In addition to heat from stoves, the walls of the Chipman house had four layers of wood planking, with an insulating paper called red rosin in between.

Sweet potatoes were a prime crop in Delaware for only a short time—by 1940, many farmers had lost their crops due to black rot, and other farmers stopped growing them due to rising labor costs. Only the sweet potato houses remained, and by the twenty-first century, just a handful of those were left.

A 2016 article noted that the sweet potato house along the Nanticoke River once used by farmer Victor Moore of Seaford had been converted into offices. Another house on a farm in Laurel had been restored and was being used for storage. Other houses, like the Chipman house and another in Bethel, were still standing but slowly falling into disrepair, despite being added to the National Register of Historic Places in 1990. In 2017 or 2018, the Chipman house was demolished and removed from the site, removing one of the few remaining links to a notable period in Delaware's agricultural history.

2
BUSINESS

Entrepreneurs and business owners have dominated Delaware for centuries. One of the most business-friendly states of the modern era thanks to its incorporation laws and specialized business courts, Delaware has a reputation for bending over backward to assist business startups, growth and expansion. We can nevertheless trace independent retail shops, superstores of yesteryear and malls among the casualties of time and the economy.

WILMINGTON DRY GOODS

One of Wilmington's cornerstone businesses for decades, the Wilmington Dry Goods store was known for its deep discounts and deeper lines. Founded in 1924 by Jacob M. Lazarus, the Dry featured permanent sales on name-brand clothes and other products, attracting customers snaking their way around the block.

Lazarus's mother and his seven siblings moved to the United States when he was sixteen. Showing his business acumen that would make him heralded as a "marketing genius," as a teenager Lazarus quickly opened multiple stores in New York State, in Witherbee, Glens Falls and Albany.

In 1924, he jettisoned the Albany location and moved to Wilmington to open Wilmington Dry Goods at 418 Market Street. It started small but

Wilmington Dry Goods was the anchor of Market Street for more than four decades. It was created from multiple smaller buildings inside. *Delaware Public Archives*.

quickly grew and was "hailed as the major spark of thriving retail business in downtown Wilmington," journalist Bill Frank wrote. "It drew thousands of customers from all economic classes of the shopping public in Delaware and nearby states." Giant ads in the newspaper didn't hurt; a former Wilmington publisher attributed his papers' success largely to Lazarus's advertising.

The Dry always closed on the Jewish high holy days—including on a day when the then-active Ku Klux Klan marched through Wilmington. "I want to be sure that the KKK knows I'm Jewish and this store is owned by Jews," Lazarus declared. He sold his stores in 1962, after nearly forty years in business, and died in 1981 in California.

Over the years, Wilmington Dry Goods expanded to the Tri-State Mall, Elsmere, Dover, Vineland (New Jersey) and Lancaster (Pennsylvania). But its Wilmington flagship store remained open until December 1978, when employees leaked the news of the imminent closure to journalists. "This is such a terrible thing to hear right before Christmas," one employee said. Unnamed workers told reporters that the building was falling apart and in need of multiple repairs—among them a broken heating system and steps that tripped shoppers.

In an open letter to Lazarus, then living on the West Coast, columnist Frank wrote:

> *It's a good thing you're in California and not here in Wilmington. You'd cry if you saw some of the conditions on lower Market Street. A few stores are opened, struggling, but for the most part, below Fourth Street, particularly, it's sad….As for King Street, I'd rather not mention conditions there. You recollect King Street on Wednesdays and Saturdays, what with the farmers' market and the bustling crowds that continued even on Saturdays to as late as 10 at night. All gone, J.M. No use weeping too much over the old days. You did your job for the town and the town did well for you.*

BURTON BROS. HARDWARE

Firefighter Ron Marvel drove the first fire engine to rescue his family's 119-year-old hardware store from the flames.

It wasn't enough.

When it opened its doors in Seaford in 1893, the Burton family's hardware store kept handwritten ledgers to document its business. Nearly 120 years later, Marvel uncovered one of those ledgers in the aftermath of the devastating fire that forced the business's closure.

The blaze on November 12, 2012, was triggered by an electric wire in a second-floor wall and caused at least $500,000 worth of damage. By January, brothers Ron and Ric had made the tough decision to shut the business down. By June, the building had been demolished.

"We pondered over all the ins and outs, what it meant to us, what it meant to Seaford," Ron Marvel told a reporter. In the end, they concluded there was too much damage to the building.

Burton Bros. Hardware was a gathering spot for many in western Sussex County, its storefront on High Street an iconic location in the city's downtown. The Marvel family had owned it since 1954, selling hardware, tools, appliances and general sundries. You could get seeds, washtubs, rope, bubblegum, coffeepots and mailboxes. The Marvel brothers let some customers run a tab. "I still enjoy when someone comes in and says, 'I need a whatchamacallit for my whosawhat,'" clerk Todd Reilly recalled.

The building was placed on the National Register of Historic Places in 1978. The west side of the store was once a movie theater. It was notable in part for the elaborate decorative sheet metal on the outside of the building, made to mimic stonework.

During their decades at the helm, the Marvel brothers were indefatigable. "I'm the janitor, the clerk, the bathroom cleaner and the check writer," Ron Marvel once told a reporter with a laugh. "Some people even think that I'm in charge."

He recalled how his grandfather Charles went to work for the founding Burton family in 1934: "They worked from 6:30 in the morning until 6:30 at night, and on Fridays and Saturdays until 11. And they would get paid in cash at 10 on Saturday night. He said he'd send his wife grocery shopping after that because places were open until midnight back then."

The Burton Hardware Store had operated in its location on High Street since around 1900. W.S. Burton leased the store to another businessperson in 1918, and his sons took it back over around 1926, making the name Burton Bros.

In the months after the fire, the Marvels finished their appliance deliveries, auctioned off inventory, salvaged what was possible and let

Burton Bros. Hardware on Seaford's High Street hadn't been owned by the Burtons since 1954, but it kept the name under the Marvel family. *Delaware Public Archives.*

Seaford Historical Society members spend three days sorting through items and documents for archives or the local museum.

The Marvels attributed their success and longevity to good old-fashioned customer service and dedication. One night, a man called just before the store closed because he needed to finish up a project before rain came. Ron stayed, opened the doors and got the customer set up and checked out forty-five minutes later. He estimated that up to 80 percent of the store's business came from repeat customers. "Customer service and the fact that we're educated on the products we're selling is the big thing," he recalled in a 2008 interview. "People are very appreciative, and that's what customer service is all about."

NINTH STREET BOOK SHOP

For four decades, book lovers flocked to Wilmington's Ninth Street Book Shop, purchasing their fill of history, novels, children's books and Delawareana. Owners Jack and Gemma Buckley, husband and wife, were beloved businesspeople whose shop many regarded as the essential core of the downtown district.

It was a sad day for readers and civic leaders alike in January 2018 when the shop closed its doors for good. Change had been coming for years, with the rise of Amazon and challenges for downtown businesses.

But the shop's history actually dates back nearly a century, before the Buckleys came on board. The late newspaper columnist and voracious reader Harry Themal traced its roots to an early 1900s print shop owned by Fred Steinlein. His wife, Alice, a bookkeeper and book lover, sold used books out of her office there. When her husband died in 1920, she made bookselling her main business, opening the Greenwood Book Shop. It was eventually located in the then new Delaware Trust Building at Ninth and Market Streets, now apartments. She later moved it to a permanent home on Ninth Street, in the Midtown Parking Center.

Joining Alice Steinlein in the business was Gertrude Kruse, who refused to sell paperbacks; she later bought out Steinlein's shares. The shop was sold to Colwyn Krussman, who later sold it to the Buckleys, owners of the Paperback Gallery.

The couple were working as public school teachers when they started the Paperback Gallery in 1977. (They ended up quitting their teaching jobs.)

Six years later, they bought the Greenwood and renamed it the Ninth Street Book Shop. Later, they closed Paperback Gallery and opened The Scrivener, which lasted just two years.

In 1994, they moved along Ninth Street to a space three times the size of the old one, growing their stock to fifty thousand books. But the building they were located in was crumbling and deteriorating, and by 2012, they had announced plans to close. An upswell of community support and a new location offered by a downtown developer let them stay open for six more years, retaining the Ninth Street name even after relocating to 730 North Market Street.

In 2017, when the Buckleys announced their final plans to close, they were selling about fifteen thousand books each year at an average of fifteen dollars each but were working sixty to seventy hours a week. Maintaining a personal touch was their goal, and they achieved it. "We didn't want to be a warehouse. We didn't want to be a coffee shop. We didn't want people to just be part of an algorithm," Jack said.

Gemma Buckley wiped tears from her eyes as she talked to a reporter about the closing. Some customers, they noted, had been regulars for thirty years. "We have no regrets. We feel like we went out on top," Jack Buckley said.

Plans were initially floated to keep the store alive by turning it into an arts venue, but those did not come to fruition. It took several more years before Wilmington proper would have a bookstore again; today, it boasts two, Books & Bagels and Huxley & Hiro.

TRI-STATE MALL

Like much of the United States, Delaware had a mall explosion in the 1960s. Plans for Claymont's Tri-State Mall were first announced in 1964, though the mall didn't open until a few years later. The indoor mall ("air-conditioned and heated") was initially proposed by Wilmington Dry Goods Co. near what would become the I-95 interchange. It aimed to draw customers from Pennsylvania and New Jersey.

Wilmington Dry, owned by a shopping mall operator since the early 1960s, already ran the Midway Shopping Center on Kirkwood Highway and operated another retail outlet on Wilmington's Market Street.

The Tri-State Mall's cinema was the only in Delaware to first show *Star Wars*. At its peak, the mall boasted 585,000 square feet of shops on 41 acres. *Delaware Public Archives*.

By 1967, initial tenants had signed on: Levitz Furniture Co., Wilmington Dry Goods, W.T. Grant and Food Fair Markets, with interest from banks, jewelry stores, clothing stores and shoe shops. A 1,400-seat movie theater was announced in late 1968 (featuring "rocker-lounger chairs" spaced out "to eliminate bothersome rising to admit other patrons to the row"). By 1970, a second screen had been added, and in 1977 a third joined its siblings. It was the only movie theater in Delaware, one of forty-five in the nation, to show a new film called *Star Wars*.

The Tri-State Mall eventually had about 585,000 square feet of retail stores on 41 acres. The complex featured an indoor-access mall, a series of stores in a strip-center format and stores on multiple stand-alone pad sites.

But by the 2010s, the mall's time had passed. Former anchors such as Levitz, Value City and Kmart had all gone under, and the mall closed its doors for good in 2015. The movie theater had closed by 1999. The strip of stores remained, including a pawn shop, a nail salon, a laundromat, a few clothes stores, Dollar General and a Save A Lot discount grocery.

By early 2023, those had all closed or moved. "For some people, this is kind of like a death," said Peter Delborrello III, co-owner of United Check

Cashing, which moved out of the strip center to Philadelphia Pike. "Your business is your child."

The only business left was Tri-State Liquors, a fixture for nearly forty years. Bolstered by a "really good long-term lease," the business owners were looking forward to a new building on the old Levitz site.

The mall site was purchased in 2021 for $12.5 million by a shopping center owner called KPR Centers. The new owner began knocking down dilapidated buildings and planning for a $50 million, 500-employee, 525,000-square-foot logistics warehouse.

Residents and public officials praised the plans. "I watched this center, this mall, just deteriorate into nothing. It really is an eyesore," one Claymonter told a newspaper. "There's a lot of people around there that do need work and it will provide what we need around here."

BLUE HEN MALL

The first indoor mall in central or southern Delaware was built in the state capital, Dover. Named in recognition of Delaware's state bird, the Blue Hen Mall opened in 1968 on eighty-nine acres near Dover Air Force Base. It was first home to Woolco, J.C. Penney's, an Acme and Braunstein's. The Dover Cinema came a year later, the first in-mall theater in the state.

A seismic shift in the market came in 1982 with the opening of the rival Dover Mall four short miles away. That began a decades-long move of the center of shopping, spreading north along US 13. By the mid-1990s, the mall was in noted decline. During 1993 and 1994, three major stores closed: first Woolworth's, then Penney's and finally Rose's. The former Dover Cinema became a concert hall and closed for good around 1998.

"The favorite sport is still memory match game, trying to recall which businesses were where," newspaper columnist Jane Brooks wrote in 1994. "A lot of Dover residents have fond feelings for the Blue Hen Mall. Like its famous namesake, it's a tough old bird."

At that time, the mall held the standard stores of 1990s-era malls, selling music, sewing notions, nutrition products and pet items. There was an optician's, a party goods store and of course the ubiquitous RadioShack.

The Blue Hen Mall's cinema was the first in-mall movie theater in the state. One of the authors fondly remembers the mall's toy store from his youth. *Delaware Public Archives.*

The owners tried to turn things around by adding state and corporate offices into transformed vacant retail space. In 1995, NationsBank announced it would be renovating eighty thousand square feet in the former Rose's store—a new anchor with more than three hundred employees. Aetna had three hundred workers in the old J.C. Penney's.

"It's amazing what you can do with $3.5 million and an empty discount store," a bank official told a business expo audience.

But those Hail Mary attempts didn't work in the end. The mall was formally converted to the Blue Hen Corporate Center, and the last of the mall stores shut their doors. At the time of this writing, occupants included Bayhealth Medical Center and the University of Delaware.

NATIONAL BANK OF WILMINGTON AND BRANDYWINE

The Bank of Wilmington and Brandywine opened its doors in March 1810 with initial holdings of $200,000 and shares to become a stockholder costing $50 each. It was one of four banks operating when Wilmington was chartered as a city in 1832; the others were the Bank of Delaware, the Wilmington Savings Fund Society and the Farmers Bank. The financial institutions were key to growth of the area, as they provided a way for merchants and business owners to secure loans to start or grow their enterprises.

Located at Second and Market Streets, the bank became part of the U.S. banking system in 1865 and added "National" to its name. Presidents of the bank included Washington Jones, a dry goods merchant and son of William G. Jones, one of the oldest businessmen in the city, and James Canby, a miller and railroad executive. George S. Capelle became a director of the bank in 1868 and president in 1888. Capelle, who lived to be ninety-four, continued as president for more than twenty years, until 1912, when the bank merged with Wilmington Trust. That merger paved the way for Wilmington Trust, founded by members of the duPont family, to become the largest in the state and one of the largest on the East Coast.

THE RIGBIE HOTEL

The 1960s in tiny Laurel were a happening time. Teenagers hung out at a youth center with a snack bar and dancing. Downtown boasted a Silco's department store, a five-and-dime, Frank Calio's shoe store, Western Auto, a fabric store and Hallmark. There were two drugstores, including Connor's, which also sold milkshakes.

One of the centerpieces was the Rigbie Hotel on Central Avenue. The original hotel on the site was known as the Cannon, destroyed in an 1890s fire and rebuilt as the Rigbie, according to local historian Kendall Jones.

Dating from the days of traveling salesmen and horse-and-buggy transportation, the Rigbie Hotel eventually transitioned into a rooming house. The bar closed and was turned into rooms as well. It was later sold and broken up into apartments and was lost to a fire in 2022.

But in its heyday, the Rigbie was a community gathering spot known for its pinochle and gin card games—as well as its pizzas, judging by stories gathered by Tony Russo for the online *Delaware Independent.*

Resident Cathy Kennard recalled the Rigbie's pizza experience: "I would order and pay for the pizza and then wait on a bench in the hallway. When the pizza was ready, someone would stick their head out the door and call to me, and I would go get it. The best part was that along with the pizza, the bartender would also give me one or two cherries. I loved those cherries!"

"It was frozen cardboard crust," onetime hardware store owner John Trivits remembered. "Frozen sauce out of a can and cheese, but everybody would die for a Rigbie pizza." Once, a group of pranksters at the bar swapped a pizza in the box for a glass ashtray filled with cigarette butts. The prankee didn't realize it until getting home and immediately went back for his pizza. "As soon as he walked in the door, everybody just roared laughing," Trivits said.

A banquet area played host to local club dinners and meetings. "It looked like, in a good way, an old grandmother's home with a lot of the woodwork and things of that sort," recalled resident Carrie Steelman. The Lions Club met there until the 1990s, hiring a high schooler to play on an upright piano during dinner. There were Christmas parties, children's pageants and Santa visits.

The bar area featured booths and bar seating for about twenty people. "You just walked in there and you were just in awe of everything," remembered Trivits. "And of course, it was old. They never remodeled or anything."

In January 2022, the Rigbie burned to the ground, displacing fifty-four residents from eleven apartments. The building's old style of "balloon construction," with no fire stop between each floor, let the blaze spread quickly, fire officials said.

HAPPY HARRY'S

Many people grew up with Harry Levin's drugstores, fiercely loyal to his smiling face and "Happy Harry" moniker. The stores became iconic for generations of Delaware shoppers—and then within a few short years faded into the past as the local chain was gobbled up by a larger chain. Such is the way of modern capitalism.

The Levin family—Harry and Diane—founded their first store, known as Discount Centre, on Marsh Road in 1962. (It was quite literally a mom-and-pop store.) The six-hundred-square-foot store did not sell prescriptions; the pharmacy didn't come around until the Levins' third store in 1965. That was the same year the name changed to "Happy Harry's Discount Drugs," as Levin the businessman embraced a marketing man's advice and the nickname customers had reportedly bestowed on him.

By 1972, the stores were doing so well they branched south out of New Castle County and established a foothold in Kent. Harry Levin was a good businessman with an eye for talent. Wanda Quesenberry recalled how he pitched her on leaving a competing drugstore to sell cosmetics for Happy Harry's over lunch at the Charcoal Pit restaurant in 1976. "Wanda, the reason I'm hiring you is because you sell, sell, sell," she remembered two decades later.

On multiple occasions, he was sued by suppliers such as Gillette or Revlon due to his discount pricing, remembered his son, Alan B. Levin. "He used to leave the suits posted at the front register so everyone could see, and they all thought that was great because he was taking one for 'them.' He had an innate ability to understand people and what they wanted, especially what Delawareans wanted."

The family business became more so in the 1980s, when Alan joined as assistant to his father. He left two years later but returned in 1986 after working on the staff of U.S. Senator William V. Roth. Alan became president of the company amid Harry's health problems.

Harry Levin died of a heart attack a year later, in 1987, while attending a drugstore conference in Michigan with Diane. He was fifty-nine. More than one thousand people attended the funeral as a sign of respect for the homegrown Delaware business leader.

"He understood Delawareans," Alan reflected on his dad's legacy years later. "That was his universe. There was never a merchant like him before, and I don't think there will ever be a merchant like him again."

Diane Levin became company chairman after her husband's death, retiring in 1992. Company president Alan Levin was no slouch at business himself, and Happy Harry's continued to grow under his leadership. And grow. And grow. In 1988, its first store in Sussex County opened, in the Rehoboth Beach area—the nineteenth all around. By 1992, its first "superstore" had launched in Branmar Plaza, and the company sold off a home medical equipment division in 1996. Retail was where it was at: The fiftieth store came to Glasgow in 2001 and the seventy-fifth to Middletown in 2005. In 2003, Alan Levin said there were no plans to sell.

That changed just a few years later, by 2006. Citing declining insurance reimbursements and pharmacist shortages as leading challenges, Alan Levin sold the chain to larger chain Walgreens, giving the new owner its first presence in the First State. By that time, Happy Harry's boasted seventy-six stores in three states—including neighboring Pennsylvania and Maryland—and did an estimated $480 million in sales. About 2,700 people worked for Happy Harry's, including 2,154 in Delaware.

The Delaware stores initially kept the local name. But by the end of 2011, Walgreen's had subsumed Happy Harry's entirely into the national chain, removing the branding and signage.

"I think Happy Harry's has always mirrored the state—a small company that has survived and thrived against some big competitors," Alan Levin said at the time of the sale. He went on to serve as state economic development director under governor Jack Markell. Diane Levin passed away in 2008, two decades after her husband.

Longtime shoppers were not so sanguine. "What is the world coming to?" customer Stacey Inglis-Baron wrote in an email to the *News Journal*. "Delawareans embrace their Happy Harry's. We don't shop at CVS or other national discount mass-merchants....First MBNA, now Happy Harry's, next Wilmington Trust, or maybe the Hotel du Pont will become a Hilton property." She had no idea how prescient her predictions would be.

Postscript: Happy Harry's may be gone, but the iconic smiling image of Harry Levin remains. A line of unofficial merchandise is being hawked by musician Aaron Fisher of Claymont—stickers, hoodies and T-shirts. The Levin family supports it. "It's great to see," Alan Levin told a reporter. "One of my nephews actually showed up in one of those shirts two weeks ago and my son also has one."

3
EATING

Dining in Delaware is a culinary experience like none other. Where else can you enjoy scrapple and muskrat along with burgers and brews? Unfortunately, some restaurants close their doors, whether due to the ravages of time, fire or retirement. The eateries in this chapter are symbols of the state's savory past worth remembering.

THE WAGON WHEEL

If you stepped into Smyrna's Wagon Wheel Family Restaurant between December and March, chances were good you were catching the aroma of freshly cooked muskrat.

The Wagon Wheel was a Kent County institution for decades, one of the few remaining places in Delaware to sell the obscure, sometimes off-putting delicacy. Muskrat platters with fried potatoes, stewed tomatoes, cornbread and dessert (fifteen dollars) drew fans from as far afield as New Jersey and Pennsylvania during the winter muskrat trapping season.

Patty and Norm Gallegos bought the Wagon Wheel from longtime owner Kitty Budd, a restaurant veteran. Under Budd's ownership, muskrat was billed on the menu as "marsh rabbit" and served in lidded dishes so as not to upset some customers' sensibilities.

Opined one customer and muskrat aficionado: "It's an acquired taste, like oysters. Look, it's not chicken. If you want chicken, eat chicken....This is muskrat. It doesn't taste like nothing else but muskrat." (Not everyone in the Wagon Wheel was there for muskrat, and not even all the employees were fans. "I'm serving it, but I don't think I'm even going to try it," said waitress Kathy Samson, a vegetarian.)

For posterity's sake, we share Budd's recipe: Soak in salt water for three days, changing the water twice daily. Parboil with Old Bay and onions for an hour. Cut into four to five pieces for serving. Brown it up with onions, salt, pepper and sage in an iron skillet. (Then, she advised newbies, "pick it up and eat it with your fingers.")

Patty and Norm followed the same recipe religiously. "That's the way Miss Kitty did it, and we just kept doing it the same way," Patty Gallegos said. She continued the tradition after head muskrat chef Norm passed away in 2007.

His death began a period of struggle for the eatery. Patty Gallegos began closing after lunch. Her granddaughter Jessica Furman, a restaurant management student, told her she couldn't close and helped apply for a TV reality show—Robert Irvine's *Restaurant: Impossible.*

The makeover in 2013 led to a revamped menu with fresher foods, including salmon, pork chops and homemade fries. (Irvine wasn't a fan of

Kitty Budd's recipe for muskrat was still in use long after she sold the Wagon Wheel. But even a *Restaurant: Impossible* intervention was unable to save it. *Delaware Public Archives.*

muskrat: "Yuk!!," he tweeted.) But the TV show and other offerings, such as a range of live music, just weren't enough. In September 2014, the Wagon Wheel closed its doors.

KIRBY & HOLLOWAY

With its iconic red-and-blue sign, Kirby & Holloway Family Restaurant lured motorists off US 13 in Dover with the promise of good food, friendly service and the off chance that they might end up eating waffles or pot roast next to a well-known politician.

The diner was opened by local sausage makers Russell Kirby and John Holloway as a counter service restaurant. At the time, decades before the construction of Delaware Route 1, US 13 was the main north–south thoroughfare in Delaware, and the founders saw a business opportunity in building a spot for a quick meal in the state capital. Kirby & Holloway, which was sold by the sausage makers to Jim Gray in the early 1980s, would later add three dining areas, a fifty-seat banquet room and, up until the 1970s, outdoor carhop service with roller-skating waiters and waitresses. In its heyday, the restaurant served as many as seventy-five meals an hour to hungry customers.

Patrons flocked to the restaurant for breakfast all day; pot roast; chicken-fried steak; burgers; a secret scrapple recipe from Russell Kirby's mother, Carrie; and homemade dinner rolls and desserts. It became a "go-to" location and tradition for travelers looking to grab a bite while making a summer pilgrimage to the Delaware beaches or while in Dover to see a NASCAR race. "It's the Cheers of Dover without the alcohol; it's where everybody knows somebody," Kent County commissioner Allan Angel told the *News Journal* in 2014. "That's our Arnold's from Happy Days right there."

Kirby & Holloway also became a Delaware landmark for political campaigning and wheeling and dealing. U.S. Senator Tom Carper first visited when he ran for state treasurer in the late 1970s; he returned many times as a congressman, governor and ultimately senator. David P. Buckson, who served as lieutenant governor in the late 1950s and did a nineteen-day stint as governor after J. Caleb Boggs resigned to become senator in 1960, was known to hold informal press conferences at Kirby & Holloway when he was seeking to regain the governor's office in the early 1970s. In 2003, presidential candidate Joe Lieberman filmed interior shots for a TV ad there during a campaign visit to Dover.

In the early hours of February 2, 2014, an electrical malfunction in the kitchen started a fire that caused more than $1 million in damage and effectively destroyed the restaurant. There was an outpouring of support for the owners and the fifty employees who were displaced, including a fundraiser that collected almost $10,000 to give to employees. The Grays promised to reopen, keeping one original section of the old building intact for nostalgia's sake. But in 2015, Jim Gray died, and plans to bring back Kirby & Holloway failed to come to fruition. City officials allowed the undamaged restaurant sign to remain, hoping that a new business would repurpose it, but in 2021, a car wash opened on the site and installed a new sign, signaling the end of a beloved Dover landmark.

THE CHUCK WAGON

The Chuck Wagon was one of those restaurants that looked like its name—an old-fashioned Conestoga wagon. The classic curved roof marked the presence of a family eatery that opened in 1952 on Kirkwood Highway. In those days, remembered Ralph Gordy Jr., whose father built the restaurant, there was barely anything on Kirkwood Highway except for fields and a few scattered businesses. "My dad said when he first put the restaurant up that a lot of people told him he was crazy. People said, 'They'll never come this far out of Wilmington to go to a restaurant.'" Back then, kids could walk across the highway for a soft pretzel and water ice; nowadays you'd be taking your life into your hands.

The business suffered some challenges. On its opening day, a car ran off the road and hit the walls. Fires were another issue, including one in 1966 and another three years later. It was also criticized by restaurant critics of the time, including Otto Dekom, who wrote: "The Kirkwood Highway is marked by many architectural monstrosities. Not the least of them is the Chuck Wagon."

The Chuck Wagon lasted as a gathering spot until the late 1980s, and the building became home to other businesses. But by the 2000s, multiple renovations had obscured the lines of the semi-western eatery that was once a local landmark—and that ultimately led to its demise. It was demolished and replaced with an Applebee's. Reporter and food critic Eric Ruth recounted: "For years, the building has been picked at and remodeled until the old structure can barely be discerned, removing much hope that it could ever be considered worthy of historic preservation." Gordy Jr. said: "Either inside or outside, there's no physical memories of what the Chuck Wagon was."

THE *NANTICOKE QUEEN*

For several decades, the *Nanticoke Queen* was one of western Sussex County's most prominent landmarks—a permanently berthed boat rising up from the banks of the Nanticoke River beside US 13.

The Seaford restaurant was a gathering place for club meetings, social events and intimate outings, a novel dining experience—aboard a ship!—unlike any other in the area.

The *Nanticoke Queen* was born in 1911 far from Delaware, to the north in Connecticut. Measuring about 130 feet long and displacing 117 tons, the wooden fishing boat was owned for many years by brothers Steven and Edward McKeever, East Coast businessmen. Known for most of its life as *McKeever Bros.*, the vessel plied its trade for several years before being commissioned into the navy in May 1917, shortly after the United States entered the Great War against Germany. Assigned to the Philadelphia naval district, it served as a minesweeper and assisted with coastal defense for the Delaware River and Delaware Bay. Eventually stationed at Cape May, New Jersey, it was sold in July 1919, with its value estimated at $47,000 or about $808,000 in 2023 dollars.

(The brothers McKeever eventually found themselves in court over the boat's sale to the federal government. They were sued by their attorneys, not an enviable position in which to be, with the lawyers saying they were promised a 5 percent commission on the $270,000 sale of three boats.)

After serving again in World War II, *McKeever Bros.* found itself back to work as a fishing boat, last used by the Otis Smith Co. in Lewes. How it ended up in Seaford as a restaurant sounds much like the children's game of Telephone. As the story goes, Salisbury, Maryland resident Lewis McBriety read about Otis Smith giving away one of his fishing boats. He passed the word on to friend Ralph Bennett of Seaford. Bennett contacted Horace

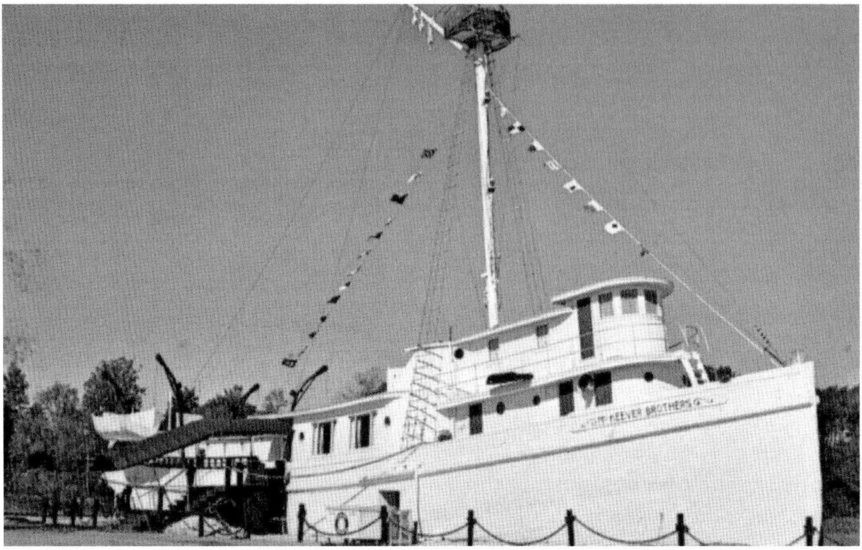

The *Nanticoke Queen / McKeever Bros.* was a fishing boat, minesweeper, coastal defense vessel and eventually a restaurant, docked permanently in Seaford. *Delaware Public Archives.*

Jones and then expanded the group to include Paul Whaley, Thayer Porter and George Sapna.

Sapna and three business partners—it's unclear from contemporary accounts which men were the official co-owners—purchased *McKeever Bros.* from Otis Smith for the princely sum of $1.

It was described as "mangy…after years of disuse" and had to be pulled and shifted into its new home by tugboats. After $200,000 in renovations, it became the *Flagship Nanticoke Queen*, opening its doors to eager local diners on August 29, 1969.

The general manager was Jack Curtis, twenty-eight, a former US Air Force navigator who had previously headed the Dover Air Force Base officers' club. To run the kitchen, Curtis brought on board a French chef, Jean Pierre Bouvier, also formerly of the Dover O-Club, and former tugboat cook Wayne Johnson. By September, the new venture was pulling in $3,800 each week (worth about $30,000 in 2023).

"It's impossible to get rid of the feeling of being on board a ship," a Wilmington newspaper writer opined. Sussex County flocked to the *Queen*, but reviewers were somewhat cooler. A restaurant critic wrote in March 1977: "Things are mostly good, but there is room for improvement." He praised the atmosphere, "resplendent with old polished wood" and "the air of elegance we associate with shipboard dining."

Just a month later, the restaurant was struck by an arson attack. The early-morning blaze, which started near a first-floor fuse box, was battled for seven hours by seventy firefighters and ten trucks, drawing resources from Seaford, Blades, Bridgeville and Millsboro.

Three dining rooms and two kitchen areas were gutted, and smoke and water damaged the upstairs lounge. The empty cash register had been forced open; authorities believed the fire may have been linked to a stolen car found nearby as well as a burglary and attempted break-in at businesses across the road. It nevertheless reopened after renovations and repairs.

In 1980, restaurant reviewer Otto Dekom—he of the earlier "room for improvement" review—returned after an Alaska family complained to the Delaware Attorney General about small portions and poor service. Lacking jurisdiction over tiny steaks, the AG referred the case to the dining critic. The verdict: "The filet on my plate was however, quite large—one might almost call it huge." The house-made cheesecake, Dekom added, "was creamy and quite good."

A few years later, the owners decided to close unless they could sell it. They found a buyer in businessman Steven C. Glenn, who got $195,000 in bond support from Sussex County to keep jobs in place. Glenn planned an extra $50,000 in improvements.

It closed temporarily in the late 1990s, lasting about a year, but was purchased by Miguel Quecada and his family, who renamed it the Nautico Seafood and Italian Restaurant. "She's the same in so many ways, but somehow different than I remembered," dining critic Eric Ruth wrote in 1999, reflecting on a youthful visit. "Maybe less grand than she seemed then (and possibly a bit more threadbare), but still a vision to behold from stern, and most certainly a dream worth waiting for."

Alas, the dream did not last. The former flagship changed hands a few more times and closed in the 2000s, leaving behind the empty hulk of a once-proud ship, which has since been removed. County records show the property was sold in 2021 for $293,000 to a Seaford company; no plans have been announced.

4
ENTERTAINMENT AND SPORTS

Where do you go in Delaware to have fun? The First State is rich with options, from movie theaters to baseball games. Some of the most treasured vanished locations are those third places (outside of home and work) where we go to relax and enjoy ourselves. Here you'll find amusement parks, music venues and two of Delaware's most storied sports teams—plus two special spots for the Black community during the days of segregation.

DIAMOND STATE DRIVE-IN

On August 12, 1949, the Diamond State Drive-In opened with a double dose of Roy Rogers in *Under California Skies* and Lyn Wilde in *Campus Honeymoon*. For forty-nine years, until it closed for good in November 2008, the drive-in on eight acres along US 13 in Felton was the site of family outings, first dates and at least one marriage proposal, not to mention showing thousands of movies.

The theater was part of a wave of drive-in openings in the 1950s. The first patented drive-in was opened in 1933 in Camden, New Jersey, by a man named Richard Hollingshead, who was looking for a way to draw potential customers to his auto parts and gas company at night. The concept caught on as an affordable hangout for families and date nights. Millie and Albert Steele bought the Felton drive-in from the original owner, W.C. Evans, in the early 1950s; according to a history of the business written by their son, the first "sound system" at the Diamond State was two twenty-four-inch bullhorns, allowing the movies to be heard from up to two miles away. The Steeles, who also lived on the property, later added the in-car speakers that would become the standard for drive-ins.

During the 1950s and 1960s, there were five thousand drive-ins in the United States. But logistical challenges made it tough to operate the theaters—they couldn't show movies in cold or inclement weather. The Steeles put on live musical shows at the Diamond State because blue laws kept them from screening movies on Sundays and also operated a roller rink on the property.

As car designs became more compact in the 1970s and 1980s, spending several hours watching a movie inside one began to lose its appeal. In

The Diamond State Drive-In opened in 1949 with Roy Rogers and Lyn Wilde and closed in 2008 with *Bolt* and *Madagascar 2*. *Delaware Public Archives.*

1966, the Diamond State, which had a capacity for 350 cars, was renamed the Hi-Way 13 Drive-In in 1966 and began showing adult films instead of family fare. The theater closed for ten years starting in 1985. In 1995, the Steeles leased the property to Don Brown, who once again began showing family movies.

The reincarnated version of the Diamond State was a success, according to Brown, but after the elder Steeles died in the summer of 2008, their heirs opted to try to sell the land, which was valued at $1.2 million, rather than renew the drive-in's lease. The drive-in's last hurrah was a showing of *Bolt* and *Madagascar 2* on November 29, 2008. The line of cars to get into the final show stretched down US 13, and patrons offered a "200-horn salute" to the theater between the two movies. A couple who had their first date at the Diamond State got engaged that night, with the proposal announced over the theater's loudspeaker.

Drive-ins enjoyed a brief resurgence during the COVID-19 pandemic, when many theaters closed due to the need for social distancing. But the next act for the land formerly occupied by the Diamond State remains to be decided—it's currently an overgrown, vacant lot, with the old screen visible to travelers along the highway. Here's to hoping for an eventual happy ending.

PUNKIN CHUNKIN

Punkin Chunkin began with a friendly argument between friends—in 1986, Sussex County residents Trey Melson, Bill Thompson and John Ellsworth planned the event as a way to settle their debate about who could design a machine that could fling a pumpkin the farthest. Three teams of contestants and a handful of spectators gathered in a field in Milton to find out the answer. Melson and Thompson won, with a catapult toss of about 128 feet.

Over the years, the event grew to include hundreds of competitors, thousands of spectators, national and international TV broadcasts, its own theme song and heavy artillery capable of sending gourds flying more than four thousand feet.

And then, at the height of the event's success, it all fell apart.

After that first informal event in 1986, the Chunkers returned in 1989 with a half-dozen competitors. There was no registration fee and no prize, really, except bragging rights. In 1991, about five thousand people came to see catapults and motorized machines take their best shot. By 1993, the event had grown to ten thousand spectators gathering on a field in Lewes to watch competitors in multiple divisions, including one for kids, one for human-powered machines and one for contraptions powered by anything short of explosives. That year, the event also won a Governor's Tourism Award for outstanding special event.

In 2002, Punkin Chunkin went national, when the competition was broadcast for the first time on the Discovery Channel; eventually, it became a staple of Thanksgiving programming on the Science Channel. As the event grew, so did the lore around it. Eventually, there were categories for pumpkins flung via air cannon, centrifugal, catapult, trebuchet, human power, human power centrifugal or torsion catapult. The machines were given intimidating names like the Big 10 Inch, Second Amendment, Second Amendment Too and Old Glory. Contestants scoured their local pumpkin patches in search of the perfect pumpkin for tossing. Chunkers aspired to beat the four-thousand-feet-plus world record set by fellow competitors and tried to avoid a "pie," or a shot that was disqualified because the pumpkin fell apart while leaving the barrel of the air cannon. Some competitors wrote a song to the tune of "Ghost Riders in the Sky" celebrating the event, and the anthem was sung during the competition's opening ceremony each day.

The event's popularity and the increasing power of the pumpkin-flinging machines forced organizers to seek larger and larger spaces to hold the event safely. A volunteer was injured in an ATV accident during the 2011 event and filed a personal injury lawsuit two years later, causing the event's host field to break ties with Punkin Chunkin. Punkin Chunkin attempted to relocate north to Dover International Speedway in 2014 and 2015, but problems with obtaining insurance led to its cancellation.

In 2016, Punkin Chunkin was set to return for three days of competition on a field in Bridgeville. The Science Channel and Discovery Channel planned to televise the event. But on November 6, the trap door of an air cannon ripped off after firing a pumpkin, sending chunks of metal into the air and critically injuring a thirty-nine-year-old woman who was working as a Science Channel producer. The television broadcast was canceled, and the woman eventually filed a lawsuit against the event, the farm where it was held and the Delaware Department of Natural Resources and Environmental Control. Although the lawsuit was eventually dismissed, Punkin Chunkin was canceled in 2017 and 2018, and organizers continued to struggle to find a suitable and insurable location.

While Punkin Chunkin was held in Illinois in 2019 and in Oklahoma in 2023, it seems likely that its pumpkin-flinging halcyon days in Delaware are never to return.

WHEELER'S PARK

Before the days of large-scale amusement parks, there were community gathering places such as Wheeler's Park. William A. Wheeler, its founder, leader and conductor, started building it in 1948, always with local children in mind. Known locally as the "Disneyland of Harrington," it actually predated Disneyland by seven years.

Admission was a dime a day. Wheeler Park boasted thirty-two separate structures for kids to climb and play on, including swinging ropes and a horse-shaped tree. There was a wading pool, a wishing well, walking trails and boat rides down Browns Branch. In later years, there were burro rides and a monkey house added. Adults could relax and entertain themselves by cooking barbecue under a pavilion or playing shuffleboard, baseball or horseshoes. A concession stand sold food. At its height, Wheeler's Park drew twenty thousand people each summer to its twenty-eight acres.

The main attraction for many young visitors was the miniature train, run by Wheeler personally. He exhorted the enthusiastic riders to scream as loud as they could to earn another ride.

Wheeler came by his railroad passion honestly: he was a freight agent for the Pennsylvania Railroad in Seaford, Bridgeville and Harrington, retiring in 1957. He was also owner of Wheeler's Radio Store, selling appliances and bottled gas. Amid failing health and eyesight, Wheeler closed the park in 1977 in his late eighties. He passed away in 1984 at age ninety-four.

Still standing are the concession stand, pavilion and wishing well. Current owners Kenny and Nicole Shinn have in recent years run a Wheeler's Park Open House to show off parts of the property to people who loved it in their youth.

BRANDYWINE SPRINGS

Long before Wilmington residents sought summer respite with a trip to the Sussex County beaches, they beat the heat by heading just west of the city to Brandywine Springs.

Beginning in the 1800s, visitors were attracted to the site because of Chalybeate Springs, an iron- and sulfur-rich mineral spring. At the time, such water sources were believed to have medicinal properties and people traveled to drink the water to cure whatever was ailing them.

In 1826, a four-story hotel was built at the site; within a few years, Greek Revival cottages were added to accommodate more visitors. Archaeologists and volunteers who have conducted digs at the site to find evidence of its past have also unearthed drawings and paintings of what the resort looked like, including men and women in fancy dress arriving in carriages or strolling the grounds.

"These were not poor people," Mike Ciosek, president of Friends of Brandywine Springs, told Delaware Public Media in 2016. "To take a vacation in the 1830s, you had to have big money. And they would come for the whole summer."

Guests left the hotel and climbed up and down a hill a few times a day to drink the restorative spring water—although Gene Castellano, who has been researching the site for decades, noted that the exercise from the walk might have been what helped guests feel better. The archaeological group has discovered that the hotel had water pumped in from a nearby reservoir and also an indoor swimming pool.

An economic downturn in the 1840s and 1850s caused the business to suffer. The hotel was rented to a boys' military school and then burned to the ground in 1853 due to a chimney fire. A second hotel was built but never reached the success of the first, until 1886, when a Philadelphia businessman named Richard Crook became the manager. The Wilmington and Western Railroad had recently been built along the edge of the property, and Crook saw an opportunity in the easy access it created for visitors.

This was the beginning of Brandywine Springs' second life as a pleasure destination. Instead of a spa for the wealthy, Crook envisioned a place where residents of nearby Wilmington could take day trips "to the country" to have a little fun.

Crook added a picnic grove, tennis courts and a small merry-go-round to the hotel grounds. Eventually, those attractions started to do better than the

An early indoor swimming pool was a feature at the original hotel at Brandywine Springs Park. It later became an amusement park and boasted of a George Washington connection. *Delaware Public Archives.*

hotel, so Crook closed it and began building out what he renamed Brandywine Springs Amusement Park. Within ten to fifteen years, Brandywine Springs featured a dance hall, a roller coaster, one of Delaware's first movie theaters, a boardwalk, games and a restaurant and food stands. There was also an elaborate Gothic entranceway, a funhouse, a three-row wooden carousel carved by Gustav Dentzel and a man-made lake called Lake Washington (likely a nod to President George Washington, who was rumored to have a Revolutionary War encampment at Brandywine Springs).

"They had these little islands in the middle, with a little pavilion and little grottos so you could take your little sweetie out there, row your boat and have a nice Sunday afternoon part of the park," archaeologist Barb Silber said.

Crook realized that access was key to the park's success, so in addition to the railway, he spearheaded the creation of his own trolley line that could bring Wilmington residents (and out-of-state travelers who initially arrived by steamboat) from the city to Brandywine Springs.

But technological progress eventually caught up with Crook, and he began to lose travelers to other destinations, including the Delaware beaches. Crook retired in 1915 and sold the park to the owners of Wilmington's other major trolley line. The trolley company owned another amusement park north of the city and began focusing investment for upkeep and advertising on that park.

"Really the great period of the amusement park was in about 1900 to 1910 and then the automobile started and people started getting cars and they could go to other places," Ciosek told Delaware Public Media. "So by 1923 it just all went to seed, just walked away. And they literally didn't open in 1924."

Brandywine Springs' amusement park was left to crumble and be scavenged by opportunistic visitors, leaving behind the foundations of some of the buildings and other more subtle signs and artifacts from what used to be there. In the 1950s, the site's history and the efforts of neighbors and volunteers helped it become Delaware's first intentional state park. Brandywine Springs became part of the New Castle County park system in the 1970s. In the 1990s, Friends of Brandywine Springs partnered with local archaeologists and started digging for more evidence of the park's past as a tourist destination. Today, the Friends of Brandywine Springs website features a detailed map of the old amusement park, along with an audio tour and historical photos.

THE STONE BALLOON

Every college town has a bar that is *the* bar, the prime gathering spot where students and townies alike come to drink beer, meet friends and new romantic partners, listen to music and make memories. For more than thirty years, for Newark, Delaware and students at the University of Delaware, that bar was the Stone Balloon.

The one-hundred-year-old building in downtown Newark was once the Washington House Hotel and later became Merrill's Tavern. In August 1971, a twenty-three-year-old former UD football player and dropout named Bill Stevenson purchased the building on Newark's Main Street with a $14,000 down payment from an inheritance from his late uncle.

After months battling with city officials over code enforcement issues, Stevenson opened the Stone Balloon, named after a club he had visited in the Virgin Islands, on February 23, 1972. Stevenson told the University of Delaware *Review* that the building could hold fifty people when he bought it; he expanded before opening by adding a second room that included a stage. Stevenson, who at the time was married to future first lady Jill Biden, described looking out the front door and seeing a line of patrons forming on the snowy opening night.

"I couldn't even tell you what happened that first night," he told the *Review* in 2006. "We closed the doors at the end of the night and I was like, 'Did that really just happen?' It was incredible to see it all be a success."

The Stone Balloon was a hit almost immediately. In a 2004 letter to the editor to the *News Journal*, Stevenson said Merrill's Tavern grossed $50,000 in all of 1970, while the Stone Balloon made more than that in just its first month. By June 1972, he announced plans for a $35,000 expansion to expand the kitchen, dance floor and bandstand, as well as adding a parking lot by demolishing two adjacent houses that he owned. Over the next few years, he built several more additions, bringing the capacity of the cavernous space to around one thousand. The bar was famous—or infamous—for its weekly Thursday "Mug Nights," when anyone who brought their own drinking glass could get beer for a dollar or less.

The Stone Balloon, photographed in 1998, was a rock destination for three decades until its closure in 2005. *Delaware Public Archives.*

In addition to becoming a go-to destination for generations of University of Delaware students, the Balloon also developed a reputation as a place to see top-tier national musical acts. Dave Matthews, Chubby Checker, Ray Charles, Hall & Oates, My Morning Jacket, Metallica, Run-D.M.C., Tiny Tim, Blue Öyster Cult, The Pointer Sisters, Joan Jett and many more all played on the bar's stage at one point.

Perhaps most famously, Bruce Springsteen played there when he was on the cusp of superstardom. It was August 13, 1974, and Springsteen was promoting his second album, *The Wild, the Innocent and the E Street Shuffle*. He played for five hours, including previewing songs from *Born to Run*, which came out the next year. In his book about the Balloon's early years, Stevenson recalled Springsteen's five encores and how the doors to the club were wide open to try to catch a nonexistent breeze on a hot, sticky summer night.

"It changed who came to Newark to perform for the next 35 years," Stevenson told the *News Journal* in 2017. "After that show, everyone wanted to be on the Balloon stage."

Stevenson convinced MTV to broadcast from the Balloon at one point; it was also named a top college bar by *Playboy* magazine. At one point, Budweiser said the Balloon was its highest seller in the country.

Eventually, however, the air went out of the balloon. Stevenson, who had some widely publicized run-ins with the law over late tax payments, sold the business in the 1980s; for a brief time, it was called the Main Street Cabaret, before retaking the Stone Balloon name in 1985. However, the club continued to rock until 2004, when the owners announced plans to demolish the local landmark and build condominiums in its place.

The last night of the old Stone Balloon was December 17, 2005, when college students and generations of former Balloon regulars came out to see Tommy Conwell and the Young Rumblers and to say goodbye. When the Washington House condominiums opened in 2009, one of the ground-floor businesses was the Stone Balloon Winehouse, with light jazz, cheese and wine tastings taking place where staff once spent hours power-washing cheap beer off the floors each night. The wine bar concept was short-lived, and after changing ownership in 2015, the space became the Stone Balloon Ale House, with an intent to celebrate the location's history and return to its roots as a bar (though now with higher-end craft beer and an extensive food menu).

"The name Stone Balloon really piques people's interest," new owner Bobby Pancake told the *News Journal* in 2015. "We want to bring back that nostalgia and give it credit for what it did and what it meant for Delaware."

THREE LITTLE BAKERS

One of Delaware's top tourist attractions, known in part for its succulent desserts, was founded by three brothers who didn't really like to bake.

Al, Hugo and Nick Immediato were born and raised in Wilmington's Italian community, where their family ran a bakery. Instead of the family business, they opted to pursue show business as an acrobatic trio called the Acromaniacs. In the 1940s, they hit the vaudeville circuit, presenting their high-flying comic act at the London Palladium, Radio City Music Hall and the Paramount. But just before they were to make a movie with Betty Grable, Nick broke his back. The other two brothers refused to replace him, and in 1948, they returned to Wilmington and opened the first of what would eventually become seven bakeries called Three Little Bakers. When they opened their fourth and, up to that point, largest store on Lancaster Avenue in 1951, the brothers said the business was turning out 50 fancy and party cakes a day on the weekdays, and up to 125 a day on Saturday and Sunday.

But the spotlight continued to beckon—the brothers continued to perform and eventually hit the road through the 1960s, always returning to the bakery operation in Delaware. Then they decided to combine their heritage with their passion, opening the first Three Little Bakers dinner theater in Kennett Square, Pennsylvania, in 1972, and then later moving to the Pike Creek Valley in 1983 with an expanded theater, plus a golf course and country club. Rather than being behind the scenes in the kitchen, the brothers were out front as hosts and the beloved public faces of the operation, who even had their own catchphrase: "That's-a-nice."

"Our father died in the bakery, our uncles died in the bakery," Nick told the *News Journal* in 1996. "It was sheer drudgery."

Three Little Bakers dinner theater was known for its expansive buffets, fancy desserts and turtle- and alligator-shaped breads. But more than the food kept people coming back: it was the elaborate stage shows and family-friendly entertainment, including Hula-Hoop contests, chorus lines, multiple rounds of the Chicken Dance and the hokey-pokey, musicals like *The Sound of Music* and national acts including Tony Danza, the Oak Ridge Boys, the Amazing Kreskin and Arneberg's Sophisticated Canines, a performing dog act that used to co-headline the Christmas show. An employee once called Three Little Bakers "Vegas in Wilmington."

It was Delaware's fifth-largest tourist destination in 1996, when Hugo said the business took in $6 million a year, including revenues from banquets, the golf course and a gift shop. At the time, Three Little Bakers employed 275 people, many of them members of the extended Immediato family. The one-thousand-seat theater was decorated with photos of the Acromaniacs with Bobby Vinton, Bob Hope, Milton Berle and the Three Stooges. Each show also included a film recounting the Acromaniacs' rise to fame.

Though Al died in 1989, Nick and Hugo continued to open the shows through the 1990s, thanking each group in the house that night, including tours, company parties, Girl Scout troops and birthday and wedding anniversary parties (each of the latter would leave with a heart-shaped loaf of bread as a souvenir). Tickets, which included a live show, an intermission performance by the Acromaniacs and a buffet plus dessert, cost $11 in 1977, rising to $50 in the 1990s.

"We're like one of them," Hugo said in 1996. "We have a friendliness people don't get out there anymore. You want somebody to take care of you, to speak to you."

Nick added: "My days on stage are not my bad days. When I'm home or on vacation, I can't find any relaxation. When I die, I want to die onstage." The brothers ran the business until 2003, when they turned it over to the next generation of family members (though they continued to remain involved).

All in all, Three Little Bakers produced about eight thousand shows, many of which sold out months or years in advance. They built relationships with tour companies that would take visitors to nearby attractions like Longwood Gardens and Winterthur during the day and end with dinner and a show. "We were the end of a beautiful day," said Vicki Immediato Winton, Hugo's daughter and Three Little Bakers' theater president, in 2009. The family also catered two to four weddings every weekend as part of a booming banquet business.

Though sales dropped in the 1990s as tastes changed and families began spending their money on home entertainment, they began a steep decline after the September 11, 2001 terrorist attacks due to drops in tourism, an uptick in gas prices and a building sense of fear of straying too far from home among senior citizens, who were among Three Little Bakers' target clientele. Shows stopped selling out, but the business had to keep paying its hundreds of employees, which caused Three Little Bakers to go into debt. Members of the family also disagreed about how the business should evolve for a new century, including whether to begin staging edgier musicals or to cut back to serving only dessert.

In March 2007, the Immediatos announced that their annual St. Patrick's Day show would be Three Little Bakers' last. The family continued to stage shows at other venues over the next couple of years, but the theater itself did not survive. The land was sold, and later, the building was torn down so the new owners could build senior care facilities where Three Little Bakers once stood. Nick died in 2013 and Hugo died in 2014, though other family members continue to work in the state's theater and restaurant communities.

But the legacy of happy memories still lives on, Winton said in 2009. "You don't find happiness in a job or in a building or in a bank account," she said. "A legacy is measured by the number of people whose lives you made better. It's measured by having a family that respects you and loves you. My father and Nick have that in spades."

KAHUNAVILLE

Before the condominiums, the movie theater, the beer garden and the museums, Kahunaville gave a shot of vitality to Wilmington's then sleepy Christina Riverfront.

Until its abrupt closing in 2006, Kahunaville was Delaware's largest nightclub and also a local landmark, due to the forty-eight-foot, smoke-spewing replica volcano at its entrance that was easily visible from I-95. Owners David Tuttleman and Robert Rosenblit started out by opening the Big Kahuna Nightclub in 1993, the same year as the opening of Frawley Stadium, home to Wilmington's minor league baseball team the Blue Rocks. They expanded with an outdoor deck and then in 1996 developed Kahunaville in a forty-five-thousand-square-foot former warehouse.

Kahunaville was more than a nightclub and restaurant—it was designed to be an experience, with a thirty-five-foot waterfall, ceiling-high fake trees, "lava rock" formations and tiki-style statues. Reminiscent of Disney, employees were referred to as "cast members." When the space opened in 1996, the owners said the Kahuna complex was already drawing 500,000 visitors a year.

The space drew local concerts, Madden tournaments and diners of all ages. Kahunaville's size and large outdoor deck also allowed the club to attract national musical and comedy acts. Bob Dylan played there, as did Green Day, Hall & Oates, Cheap Trick, the Beach Boys, Collective Soul, Shaggy and Warren Zevon. Legend has it that comedian Artie Lange accidentally kicked a poinsettia plant into a female fan's face during a Christmas show.

For a while, Wilmington's Kahunaville was the "flagship" of an international conglomerate of restaurant-nightclubs. In 1997, the owners opened a second location in Langhorne, Pennsylvania, followed by locations in Nevada, New York, Massachusetts, Michigan, Ohio, New Jersey and Florida. Kahunaville went global in 2002, when the company signed a territorial licensing agreement with a Korean hospitality company, which planned to open three locations in five years. A group of US employees traveled to Korea to help open the first location.

But eventually, growth—both the company's and the Christina Riverfront's—got the best of Kahunaville. Several locations closed, and others were sold to help alleviate the company's debt. In 2006, owner Tuttleman surprised customers, employees and city officials by closing the Delaware club's doors with just a day's notice. He told the local newspaper that Kahunaville had become "a victim of our own success," with noise complaints and problems with parking increasing as new condos, offices and other businesses brought more people to the Riverfront.

Since the nightclub's closure, Tuttleman has hosted two Kahunaville "reunions" at other local venues. "I remember the crowds, the joy and the fun," he said before the second in 2018. "I can still hear the music and feel the people." And the Kahunaville space continues to play a role in the Riverfront's vitality. Though the volcano was taken down due to structural concerns (and displacing at least one groundhog), the building reopened in 2009 as the Delaware Children's Museum.

JASON BEACH

On the north side of Trap Pond State Park, a finger-like point juts into the murky waters. For several decades, the area was known as Cypress Point, an homage to the trees that grow from the pond's depths. But that label replaced an earlier name for that part of the state park, whitewashing part of Sussex County's history.

During the 1950s and 1960s, that section of the Laurel-area park was known as Jason Beach—a Black resort area on government property during the days of segregation. Across the pond, the beach near the park headquarters was for white residents; Jason Beach was for Blacks. Segregation was not mandated by state law but was the practice nonetheless.

Jason Beach bears its name to honor educator and pastor R. William C. Jason, president of what is now Delaware State University, which he led for twenty-seven years. The name dates back to the state's acquisition of the parkland in 1951.

Both swimming areas featured picnic shelters and tables, toilet facilities, a bathhouse and fireplaces, but separate and unequal was the general rule. In 1957, Jason Beach's food concession was valued at $150 while the white beach's was worth $1,130. A concrete pad at Jason Beach today is the only remainder of the A-framed "snack shack" concession stand run by local grocers Andrew and Agnes Selby, who sold sandwiches, sodas, candy and snacks.

In 1962, a Sussex newspaper reported that Jason Beach was being underused due in part to its facilities being in poor repair, noting crumbling fireplaces, poorly kept buildings and the lifeguard stand missing a platform.

Still, Black residents gathered for religious services and baptisms as well as dancing and fun. A jukebox played jazz and James Brown. "When you went to Jason Beach, you had the chance to meet your friends, your cousins and what have you, and you met people that you'd never seen before," recalled resident Howard West. "It was really a meeting place."

"The white kids played over there [across the pond], and we played over here," remembered Laurel town councilman Jonathan Kellam, a former newspaper reporter. "One of the biggest questions we had was, 'I wonder if they're having as much fun over there as we're having over here.'"

New attention came to the de facto segregation in the summer of 1963. "Race Troubles Ripples Placid Trap Pond," the *Delaware State News* declared. For a decade, the Red Cross had given swimming lessons to children coming from western Sussex towns. Each town had a particular week. In July, three buses carrying about sixty Black children from Seaford arrived at the park on a week set aside for Laurel children and were turned away. The next day, the Seaford children came back and swam at the white swimming area, not across the pond at Jason Beach.

The ensuing uproar triggered a two-day cancellation of swimming lessons and sparked headlines in the local papers. Park leaders and Red Cross instructors alike insisted that the issue was not racial discrimination but simply geographic turn-taking. "If those Negro children had shown up when it was the Seaford area's turn for the lessons, they would not have been turned away," declared state parks chairman Thomas W. Murray Jr.

The parks agency had to issue a statement decrying segregation and reiterating that anyone may "use fully the recreational facilities provided, maintained and administered with state funds and under state auspices." Separation of the beaches was officially ended with the 1964 Civil Rights Act.

Over time, the name Cypress Point came to replace the label of Jason Beach. But in 2022, the state restored the name to that part of the state park, erecting a historic marker and interpretive signage to commemorate the history of the place so special to the Black community.

ROSEDALE BEACH

Rosedale Beach was once described as Delaware's Fort Lauderdale of the 1940s—a resort and entertainment venue that was always swinging. But it was mostly known as a place where both Blacks and whites could relax and enjoy music and culture in the days of segregation.

The known history of Rosedale Beach goes back to the early 1900s, when nine acres of land owned by Isaac Harmon was turned by his son, Noah, into a recreation area known as Noah's Park. Located on Indian River Bay near Millsboro, it was known for baseball, swimming and religious meetings. A five-room hotel also operated there from the early 1900s. The site was sold in the early 1930s to a couple named David (Dale) and Rosetta Street; local lore says they combined their names to create the new moniker of Rosedale Beach.

The Streets constructed a dance hall at Rosedale where predominantly Black performers from around the country came. In 1937, it was sold to Jesse and Floyd Vause, who built a thirty-two-room hotel by 1946. The Vauses put up a boardwalk, baseball fields and a merry-go-round. There was a hotel bar, the Young Man's Republican Club, for GOPers only. (The Republican Party was different back then.) It was included in the Green Book, noting welcoming places for Black travelers prior to desegregation, and also hosted Saturday night barn dances for visiting hunters.

Performers at the dance hall included renowned names such as Aretha Franklin, Louis Armstrong, Miles Davis, Duke Ellington, Fats Domino, Ray Charles, Ella Fitzgerald, Cab Calloway, Count Basie and a young Stevie Wonder.

Doris Price, who grew up at nearby Millsboro, remembered hearing Fats Waller perform when she was around five from a nearby hill. "My mother and father never went in the dance hall and they didn't drink, but they

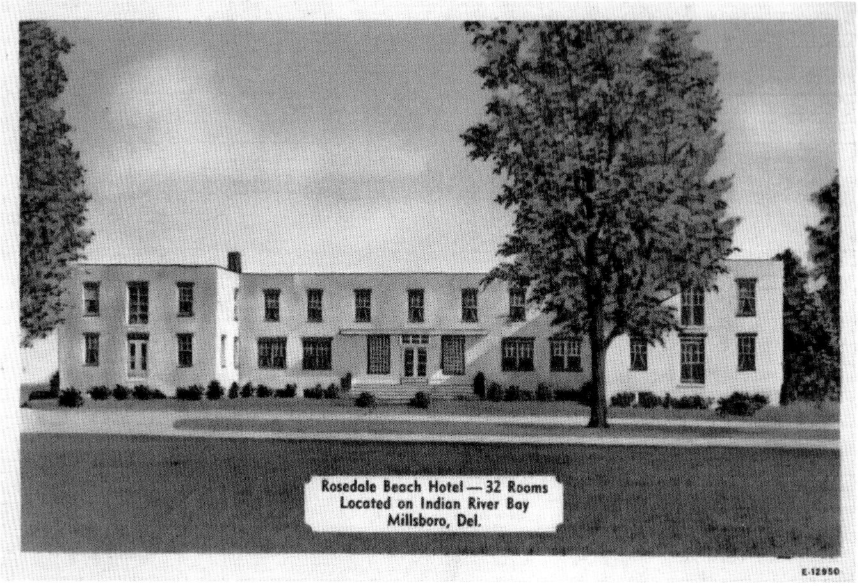

"Rosedale was an oasis," recalled Delaware State football player Don Blakey. It was open in its modern incarnation from the 1930s to the 1960s. *Delaware Public Archives.*

socialized," said Price, who is of mixed race. "We were down there visiting and we could hear the music."

In 1954, Don Blakey was a football player on the Delaware State College team. He and classmates went down to Rehoboth Beach and worked short-term jobs in the hotels and beach businesses, and after getting off work nights they would sometimes stay over at the resort. "Rosedale was an oasis, with all kinds of activities going on. It was like we had been in the desert—tired, thirsty, disheveled—and all of a sudden we saw this place in the distance where we could relax and be taken care of," said Blakey, who went on to become a noted Black educator and state legislator.

Much of what we know about Rosedale is due to the research of Tamara Jubilee-Shaw, who studied Rosedale for a historic marker that was erected in 2011. Her father, Leroy Jubilee, told her of his experience at Rosedale: "I used to sneak in the back door to hear the music and strummed on my guitar just like the musicians on stage there. Fancy yachts would ride by so the passengers could listen to the thumping and swinging sounds coming from the hotel."

But Rosedale's fortunes declined after desegregation in the late 1950s, as more public venues became open to people of all races. The lack of air-conditioning also hurt bookings in the hotel. The storm of 1962 wiped out the boardwalk. The resort went bankrupt and was sold at sheriff's sale in 1962; it reorganized in 1963 but just operated as a regular hotel. Bands played and the bar remained open until 1981, when it closed. Rosedale was sold to developers in 1983 and is now home to condos called Gull Point.

THE CLIPPERS

Like many innovative ventures in Delaware's history, the Wilmington Clippers' story begins with a du Pont—Lammot du Pont II, who founded and funded the football team throughout its span. Started as a minor-league team, the Clippers brought professional football to Delaware for a highly satisfying run that included a national championship.

The Clippers kicked off their first season in 1937 against the Philadelphia Eagles. More than four thousand fans were on hand, paying $2.50 for box seats. Unfortunately, the Clippers lost their first outing, 14–6.

The team was founded as an independent one but joined the American Association in 1939. Nicknamed "the Fleet," the management used its cash on hand liberally. Former NFL ringers received high pay to join the squad. But despite strong fan support, "the Clippers lost plenty of Lammot du Pont's money," historian Doug Gelbert recorded.

One notable name that first season with the Clippers was a player out of Fordham named Vince Lombardi. He played in the Clippers' first win, over the Richmond Arrows 25–7, and started in five games in 1939. Lombardi then departed the Clippers to go on to a highly successful career in coaching.

The teams' largest crowd was in the 1939 season opener against the Brooklyn Dodgers, a National Football League team. In 1940, they beat the Philadelphia Eagles 16–14, the first time an American Association team had whooped an NFL team. And they won the championship in 1941 over the Long Island Indians.

A noteworthy game was against a squad of soldiers from Fort DuPont in November 1941, a month before the United States entered the war. The game helped fund the USO and Fort DuPont's education and recreation accounts. The soldiers were coached by "one of the Clipper greats of past seasons," Lieutenant Charles R. "Tod" Goodwin, and had gotten seven weeks of practice and coaching, a Wilmington newspaper scribe wrote. Fellow former Clipper Siggy Andrusking, now in the army, played for Fort DuPont. "They fully expect to give the Wilmington pros trouble," the *Morning News* wrote in a preview.

In anticipation of a good game, more than 4,500 people were on hand for the matchup in Wilmington Park to watch the soldiers lose. The team of former college and professional stars, bolstered by some high school and prep players, were "game but overpowered," in Gelbart's words. The Clippers tromped them 34–0. A newspaper photo shows Clipper back Les Dodson weaving deftly through a field of his teammates and opponents lying on the ground. The game was filmed by Fox Movietone News.

But as was foreshadowed by Goodwin and Andrusking's enlistments in the armed forces, the U.S. entry into World War II the next month pulled men off the gridiron and hampered much of the sport. The American Association suspended play in 1942, though the Clippers continued with du Pont's support. Without much opposition, the Fleet were one of the strongest non-NFL teams in 1942, winning with blowout box scores like 77–0. A rematch against the Eagles saw a tie game, 21–21.

The Clippers played an exhibition game against the servicemembers of Fort DuPont in 1941, with proceeds going to uniforms. *Delaware Public Archives.*

With the war raging, the Clippers suspended play from 1942 to 1946, when they returned as a farm team of the Washington football club. They were outscored that year 184–47, and it went downhill from there. They reached the 1949 playoffs but lost to Richmond 66–0. Lammot du Pont pulled the plug before the start of the 1950 season, and the reign of the Clippers was over.

THE WILMINGTON QUICKSTEPS

The original Wilmington Quicksteps were a top-caliber baseball team in the First State in the late 1800s, known as "Delaware's team." Baseball of the early era was a scattered sport, with games played against both pro and amateur teams. Formed in the early 1870s, the Quicksteps won several early games and with them acclaim as the state's leading team. A revitalized and reorganized Quickstep squad in 1873 "within a short time became the strongest baseball club to yet represent Wilmington," historian Doug Gelbert recounted.

They were undefeated against local teams and played against squads from Georgetown and Milford to earn the self-sobriquet "Champions of the Peninsula." They triumphed against the Wilmington Maple Leaf for the 1875 state championship, winning 24–4. In August, the Quicksteps battled the Chicago Whitestocking—their first professional matchup—falling 11–4. They outran the Philadelphia Athletics 6–4 and the Diamond State team 26–4 and gave themselves another honorific, that of the "Champion Amateur Nine of the United States."

At one point in the 1870s, there were two Quickstep teams: one professional in the National Professional Association, and one amateur, known as the Quickstep Amateurs. While amateurs of the time were unpaid, the professionals were paid ten dollars a week and wore white uniforms with a red belt and blue stockings. A seven-game competition of Quicksteps versus Quicksteps opened before 1,200 fans, with the pros taking the win, 11–6.

In the end, it was difficult to make enough money at the business of baseball in the 1870s. "While Wilmingtonians were still greatly interested in baseball," Gelbert wrote, "they weren't interested in paying for it. A typical Quicksteps game would draw about 500 paying customers but twice that would gather on the hills, rooftops and wagons around the park." The Quicksteps disbanded ahead of the 1877 baseball season, and an attempt to bring them back that July fell short.

The Quicksteps were revived in the 1880s. By 1884, backed by manager Joe Simmons and President John T. West, "Wilmington swung hard, threw hard, and ran hard," historian Jon Springer wrote in his book about the Quicksteps. "They weren't gentlemen on their field but warriors who attacked their opponents [and] snapped back at umpires."

The team was made up of mostly first-generation Americans of Irish descent. There were at the time four professional leagues: the American Association, the National League, the Eastern League and the Union Association. The Quicksteps were part of the Eastern League, alongside the Baltimore Monumentals, the Richmond Virginians and the Trenton Trentonians. (Creativity abounded in New Jersey in those days.) The Quicksteps made their mark, leading the league 16–6 by Memorial Day, outscoring their foes 259–119.

But after switching leagues and joining the Union Association, several top players left for other teams, including Oyster Burns and Dennis Casey heading to Baltimore. The team fell apart on the field and lost game after game. The result? The Quicksteps had a final record of two victories and sixteen losses, an astoundingly embarrassing winning percentage of .111. Players scattered to Kansas City, Philadelphia and Newark, and the Wilmington Quicksteps were left in defeat.

5
INDUSTRY

From logging to brewing and milling to manufacturing, making things is part of our DNA. Delawareans made early innovative cars, sifted the finest "superfine" flour and built ships that sailed our waterways and oceans. With time and progress, these early industries have fallen by the wayside—but we remember them all the same.

THE CYPRESS SAWMILL AT TRAP POND

The story of Trap Pond—the three-hundred-year evolution of a human-built pond into a popular recreation area—is an excellent example of how Delaware's early industry fundamentally changed the character of the land.

In the 1700s, when early European colonists began moving to the region, the Trap Pond area was simply a swamp. It wasn't until the American Revolution that men began damming streams and creating ponds—known as millponds—to float newly logged trees out of the dense stands deep into the swamps. Trap Pond owes its existence to such early entrepreneurs; a sawmill soon followed to shape the raw timber and prepare it for transport. This was far from unique. By the 1820s, up to twenty different millponds were created in the greater Laurel area between Trap Pond and Broad

Creek. Builders coveted the bald cypress trees that came out of the Trap Pond swamps. Many houses bore cypress shingles, largely impervious to rot and insect pests.

Gradually, farming replaced logging as the dominant business type in the area, and the Trap Pond sawmill became an innovative gristmill, grinding corn and wheat into meal and flour for farmers in the area. Further innovation was to be the mill's downfall, however. As the railroad came to Laurel, farmers switched from grain and corn to fresh fruits and vegetables that could be easily transported on the rail lines, such as watermelon, peaches and strawberries—more perishable, certainly, but also with more profit potential. The mills fell into disuse, and many in the area had washed away by the early 1900s.

At Trap Pond, the man-made dam washed out in 1931 after a flood, leading to a draining of the pond. In 1936, the federal government purchased the property, and the New Deal's Works Progress Administration went to work. The government blew stumps out with dynamite, poured sand on the bottom of what would become the new swimming area and relocated and rebuilt it on the eastern side of the pond.

Trap Pond began as a sort of business incubator, with mills such as this cutting wood and grinding corn and wheat. Many had gone under by 1900. *Courtesy Delaware State Parks.*

By 1941, residents were heralding the transformation of the site, called "Trap Park" by one newspaper, into a popular federally owned destination featuring picnic areas, a bathhouse and a softball field. In 1951, the state purchased the property, and it became Delaware's first state park, the place where multiple generations of Sussex County residents learned to swim. (In 2000, the swimming area was closed permanently. The pond's water quality was so impaired that swimmers complained of rashes or illnesses, and the park had problems finding qualified lifeguards.)

BANCROFT MILL

Constructed to take advantage of the power of the Brandywine River, the Bancroft Mill grew from a small cotton mill that provided the fiber to New York and Philadelphia in the 1830s to a worldwide operation that provided fashions to none other than Miss America.

An English textile weaver named Joseph Bancroft opened the mill, which is located just west of downtown Wilmington on land that is adjacent to what is now Alapocas Run State Park, in March 1831. The company would ultimately remain in the Bancroft family for 130 years. Joseph's sons, William and Samuel, joined the business in the 1840s, and the mill grew rapidly during the Civil War when the United States was largely closed to imports from England. After the war, the Bancrofts developed a new bleaching process and switched their focus to finishing cotton cloth. They incorporated the company as Joseph Bancroft & Sons on October 1, 1889, when it was described as the largest textile finishing plant in the country.

By the mid-1930s, Bancroft Mill was producing its own line of rayon clothing called "Ban-Lon" and a cotton finishing process known as "Everglaze." Both were licensed in Europe and the United States, leading to foreign royalties accounting for more than 70 percent of the firm's total profits by the 1950s. Bancroft became a division of New York–based Indian Head Mills in 1961.

From 1953 to 1967, Bancroft was a sponsor of the Miss America pageant and used the annual event to promote its custom lines of fabrics. Miss America appeared in fashion shows modeling Everglaze and Ban-Lon apparel, which also included clothing for men and children. Consumers could buy patterns to make their own version of the clothes and purchase

Founded in the 1830s, Bancroft Mill eventually faltered under competition pressure from the South and overseas. Its owner went bankrupt in 2003. *Delaware Public Archives.*

clothing, draperies, upholstery and bedding under the Everglaze and Ban-Lon labels at department stores.

But as it became cheaper to produce textiles in the South and later overseas, Bancroft and other mills in the Northeast fell into a decline. Bancroft was put up for sale by Indian Head in 1972 and purchased by a group mostly made up of department heads from the mill. The property changed hands multiple times from the 1980s until 2003, when current owner the Wilmington Piece Dye Company went bankrupt. Despite being added to the National Register, the complex was vacant and abandoned for years. Parts of the empty mill structures were ultimately destroyed by fires, most recently in 2016.

It was also around that time that the land attracted the eye of developers. While the power of the Brandywine was no longer the best way to manufacture textiles, the scenic river view was a selling point for apartments and condominiums. Some of the developments have used portions of the former mill structures. To make way for the most recent housing development, in fall of 2017 the 230-foot mill smokestack was imploded, ending more than 180 years of history in less than 10 seconds.

SUPERFINE BRANDYWINE

In the 1600s, the first mill on the Brandywine was opened by Swedes, the family of one Tymon Stidham, for milling barley. In the next century, around 1720, Samuel Kirk bought the old mill from the Stidhams and formed the Kirk Company. In 1743, Oliver Canby came on the scene and bought out the company. He eventually ran three mills and controlled an excellent portion of the Brandywine. His plan was to purchase wheat from the growers and then sell the flour himself, a change from the past practice of grinding flour for farmers to take back to their homesteads. Those holdings would underwrite Canby fortunes for generations to come.

The prime product of the Brandywine mills was "Brandywine superfine," top-quality flour that for a time could not be rivaled. Superfine flour was the "whitest, lightest, and finest flour," historian Carol Hoffecker recounted. More coarse grades were called middlings, then ship stuff, followed by shorts. The technology of local genius and inventor Oliver Evans both saved in labor costs and allowed millers to reprocess the middlings to produce more superfine flour, an increase of 3–4 percent—thus improving the Evans mills' profitability.

The millers of the Brandywine reached their maximum dominance after the Revolutionary War. They bought grain from Delaware, Maryland, New Jersey and Pennsylvania, and the flour that came from their mills "was the most sought-after flour in the American market." The millers' family names are still prominent in Delaware: Marshall, Tatnall, Lea. As late as the 1870s, short statements in the *Delaware Tribune* recounted the price per bushel of Brandywine superfine.

The merchant millers prospered in early Delaware in the area known as Brandywine Village, in those days outside of the Wilmington city limits. Today, that community stands in the heart of Wilmington by the Brandywine Zoo.

LEA MILLS

Another mill of note in Brandywine Village was that of Thomas Lea. Actually made up of several gristmills run by Lea and his father-in law, Joseph Tatnall, the mill complex included ones along the Brandywine River and Red Clay Creek. One visitor to the United States in 1795–96 said about Thomas Lea,

> *He is also a Quaker, about thirty years of age; he is a handsome, cheerful, active man. Like a true American patriot, he persuades himself, that nowhere is any undertaking executed so well, or with such ingenuity as in America.... They purchase their corn in Virginia, Maryland, and in the state of New York, which is brought from thence in two of their own ships; they convert it into flour; and the same sloops carry it back again to Philadelphia, where it is sold for exportation.*

One of the mills burned down in 1819, leading to the destruction of three thousand bushels of wheat and four thousand bushels of corn. It was rebuilt after Thomas Lea's death in 1824 by his son, William Lea. William and his sons later ran all of the Lea and Tatnall mills on the Brandywine; they renamed the company William Lea & Sons Co., in 1864. That enterprise operated for many years, until about the 1920s. The exact year they stopped grinding flour is not known. The city purchased their water rights in 1923, and the property was sold in 1928. The Wilmington Academy of Art and the Wilmington Drama League occupied parts of the buildings for some time.

In 1931, artist Frank Schoonover was commissioned to create an oil painting of Lea Mills for Alice Lea Spruance. He even added a small black dab of paint on the dock, "making the picture authentic right down to the rat," noted one museum.

Located in the Brandywine Village neighborhood, William Lea & Sons was formed in 1864. The property was sold in 1928. *Delaware Public Archives.*

DUPONT MOTORS

The DuPont name is linked in Delaware business lore to gunpowder and chemicals. The family's venture into automobile production is more obscure, though just as fascinating.

The duPont Motor Manufacturing Company, or duPont Motors, was founded by scion E. Paul duPont in 1919 after the conclusion of the Great War. The firm got up to speed fairly quickly. An announcement was made in July 1919, and by November the first model was shown at a New York auto exhibition, attracting significant interest.

The duPont car plant was located on Wilmington's Commerce Street at Dock Street, which remains an industrial area today. The company was headquartered at 904 Market Street, the future location of the Delaware Trust Building.

The chassis was built first, with the motor assembly awaiting construction of a 250-by-60-foot machine shop. The first car featured a 4-cylinder engine, a 125-inch wheelbase and 4-speed transmission. Weighing 3,150 pounds, it was projected to go on sale for $3,500—about $56,000 in today's dollars. The engine, a newspaper reported dutifully, "when wide open will show a speed of much better than a mile a minute."

There were two models produced at first, a touring car seating four to five passengers and a runabout with a shorter wheelbase. Plans were being discussed for a 6-cylinder car in the future. By year two, three models were being developed: a touring car, roadster and a closed car.

"It is the plan of the company to make the design and construction of this car conform to the best standards of American and European practice," a correspondent wrote in the pontificating style of the day. "Within a year Wilmington will probably have another flourishing major industry," another writer declared.

DuPont Motors was led by Paul duPont as president, Arthur M. Marie as vice president and general manager and John A. Pierson as chief engineer. By the fall of 1920, the company had apparently outgrown its Wilmington plant and announced plans to move its manufacturing operation to Moore, Pennsylvania, where it would be able to produce 150 cars a month. The new plant would be on 8.5 acres, measuring 790 by 75 feet paralleling the rail line. The entire 1920 year's product—500 cars—had already been claimed by distributors as of May, with the first sold to an Atlanta dealer in November 1921. The Moore plant eventually closed, and production had moved back to Wilmington by 1924.

DuPont Motors was in business for just twelve years, its production line felled by the Depression. The owner personally test-drove each new car for ten days. *Courtesy of Hagley Museum and Library.*

DuPont Motors eschewed the modern assembly line, building each car on a custom basis. It produced an average of 44 cars per year over its twelve-year life—537 vehicles in total. "Du Pont sought perfection and not a mass market," a later newspaper reporter would write: Paul du Pont personally test-drove each car for up to ten days.

Then the Depression came, and duPont Motors shut down; custom luxury cars were not selling in a nation beset by poverty. By February 1931, an advertisement in a Wilmington newspaper declared: "FOR SALE OR RENT: The Modern Plant / du Pont Motors Company," with twenty-one-thousand-plus-square feet of space that could be subdivided among "responsible tenants."

Paul du Pont's interests shifted, and he took over the Indian Motorcycle Co. Indian later went bankrupt under subsequent leadership, but, wrote historian Allan Girdler, "if it hadn't been for Paul du Pont, the Harley guys almost surely wouldn't have had anybody to feud with."

NEWARK CHRYSLER PLANT

The roots of Chrysler's Newark assembly plant stretch back to the late 1930s, when the automaker bought sixty-five thousand acres of land just south of downtown to use as a parts depot. A few days before Christmas 1951, news broke that Chrysler would break ground on what was billed as "one of the two largest medium tank building plants in the nation." Initial plans for the plant called for one million square feet of floor space to employ between three and four thousand workers. At the time, due to a tight labor market and housing shortage, there were concerns about where the workers would come from and where they would live. But ultimately, the Chrysler assembly plant turned into an economic engine that employed generations of Delawareans in high-paying jobs with benefits, with a peak employment of more than five thousand people in the 1960s.

When the Korean War ended in 1953, Chrysler began phasing out the plant, potentially imperiling the three thousand workers there. But within five years, the plant had been converted for automaking, beginning with Plymouths, the first of which rolled off the assembly line on April 30, 1957. The plant produced sixty-seven thousand cars during its first year. By 1959, employment had reached 4,300. A second shift was added at the plant in 1964, the same year General Motors added a second shift at its nearby plant on Boxwood Road in Wilmington.

In 1969, eighteen-year-old Bill Mariano left home in West Virginia to escape working in the mines by joining his uncle Joe in Delaware, working on the assembly line at Chrysler. "I was going to do something different than coal mining and make a better living," Mariano, who ultimately worked for Chrysler for thirty-six years, told the *News Journal* in 2007. "I doubled my pay and worked in a nice, clean environment. To me, I was in heaven." Workers like Mariano, who moved to the area due to the promise of higher wages and union benefits at Chrysler, helped expand middle-class neighborhoods in Newark and throughout New Castle County. Mariano raised his family working at Chrysler, and then his two sons eventually worked there.

Chrysler produced a number of different cars at the plant, including the Valiant and the Dodge Dart in the early 1960s; K-cars, the Plymouth Reliant and Dodge Aries in the 1970s; the Dodge Spirit and Plymouth Acclaim in the 1980s; the Chrysler LeBaron, Dodge Intrepid, Chrysler Concorde and Eagle Vision in the 1990s; and the Dodge Durango in the 2000s. The

Delaware's Chrysler Plant began producing tanks and switched to Chrysler, Plymouth and Dodge vehicles in 1957. The site is now a University of Delaware tech and science campus. *Delaware Public Archives.*

millionth car rolled off the assembly line at the plant in 1965, and by 1978, 5,500 people worked there.

But beginning in the 1980s, workers began to face new uncertainties, as car production moved south and overseas. Chrysler was saved from bankruptcy in 1980 thanks to $1.2 billion in loan guarantees from the federal government; Delaware was the first state to approve aid for Chrysler, with then governor Pete du Pont proposing a $5 million loan. Chrysler threatened to close the plant in 1987 due to a labor dispute; a new contract was ultimately signed, and over the next seventeen years, Chrysler spent millions to retool the plant for new car models.

The Newark plant was assembling Dodge Durango and Chrysler Aspen SUVs in the mid-2000s, when rising gas prices, a slowing economy and a credit crunch created a shift in consumer tastes toward smaller vehicles. Rumors began to swirl that the plant would close. Those rumors proved true on February 14, 2007, when Chrysler announced a major restructuring plan that included dropping the Newark plant, which then employed about two thousand people, down to one shift later that year, and then idling the plant in 2009. In the interim, Chrysler said it would begin assembling the fuel-efficient version of the Durango in Newark, causing some to hope the plant might ultimately remain open.

"We have another day to fight," then-Senator Joe Biden said, giving the plant a 50-50 chance of surviving. "This is not over."

But sales and the economy continued to slump, and on October 23, 2008, Chrysler announced it would close the Newark plant early. At the time, about 1,100 people worked there. The closure was announced at a 6:45 a.m. all-hands meeting at the plant.

"We've been expecting it for a while," Marcy Watkins, a twenty-eight-year plant employee, told the *News Journal*. "We just weren't expecting it to come the way it came. We had no warning it was coming today." Chrysler's decision came as the GM plant in Wilmington announced it would eliminate one shift at that plant and Invista announced layoffs at its nylon plant in Seaford. The Chrysler plant was the city of Newark's largest single property taxpayer, and with suppliers for the plant located throughout the region, the decision was expected to have numerous ripple effects.

The University of Delaware bought the 272-acre site in October 2009 for $24.25 million with plans to build a research park called the Science, Technology and Advanced Research (STAR) Campus. The new campus now houses health science clinics, a research and development center for vehicle-to-grid technology, a biopharmaceutical innovation center and more than thirty private companies.

Most of the original plant complex is gone, but part of the original brick and a hand-painted mural of Chrysler cars were preserved. During a tour for former employees in 2015, former plant manager Jim Wolfe noted that the name "STAR" campus was derived in part from Pentastar, Chrysler's former logo. "If you look at this place, it's alive again," Wolfe said.

BOXWOOD ROAD

The news outranked the battle for Okinawa and the bombing of Toyko. "GENERAL MOTORS TO BUILD PLANT HERE," the Wilmington newspaper proclaimed in giant front-page type in 1945. The one-million-square-foot plant was projected to hire about three thousand workers to start. As part of the company's postwar expansion, it would build in Wilmington, Kansas City and in Columbus, Hamilton and Sandusky, Ohio. (Why set up shop in Delaware? The favorable business climate was perhaps one element, but another factor may have been that the DuPont Co. owned almost a quarter of the automaker.)

Over the decades, the plant on Boxwood Road produced a whole panoply of vehicles. Designed originally to make Buicks, Oldsmobiles and Pontiacs, it also turned out Impalas, Chevettes and Saturns. The first car off the line was a 1947 Pontiac. At its peak in the mid-1980s, more than five thousand employees labored there.

"You could see the parking lot was full, you knew people were working, and they were contributing to the economy," remembered retiree Steve Quindlen, who worked there for forty-one years. "You could see [the cars] go on a car carrier or reshipped by rail, and they'd go out the door on a daily basis."

GM survived recessions and downturns and layoffs, even as multiple generations went to work there in good-paying union jobs. There were warnings over the years, to be sure. In 1992, a permanent closure seemed imminent but was reversed. In the mid-2000s, Boxwood Road was the sole production line for the Pontiac Solstice, Saturn Sky, Opel GT and Daewoo G2X, and things appeared stable for a while.

They weren't. The announcement of the plant's closing in June 2009 hit Delaware like the deep peal of a bell, following on GM's bankruptcy filing. The world's second-largest auto manufacturer was closing eleven plants by July, putting 550 Delaware workers on the street and telling another 515 previous layoff victims that they would not be coming back. "The hope drained away when GM left," recalled current County Executive Matt Meyer. "We've certainly had the wind knocked out of us in the last few months," said Alan B. Levin, Delaware's economic development chief under then governor Jack Markell, reflecting on the closure of the Chrysler plant as well. When the last car went off the line, workers lined up to sign the silver Pontiac Solstice.

The massive plant was three million square feet on more than 140 acres. Who would be interested in an industrial site built right after World War II?

But behind the scenes, the state was hurriedly soliciting ideas, talking with businesses and putting its most appealing package together. A savior was riding to the rescue in the unlikely form of Henrik Fisker. Later that year, his company announced a plan to purchase the site and save 2,500

Delaware's General Motors plant produced Pontiacs, Buicks, Oldsmobiles, Chevettes, Impalas and Saturns over the decades. *Delaware Public Archives.*

jobs by converting the GM production lines into a center for building up to 100,000 electric plug-in cars each year. It took Delaware two months and two days to complete the deal, Levin recalled. The plant itself had been shut down in a way that would assist new owners with starting up; the paint shop in particular would have cost $250 million to $350 million to build from scratch.

Needless to say, the Fisker dream did not materialize. Boxwood Road would never again make cars. After its battery supplier folded, Fisker also filed for bankruptcy and the deal fell apart. Chinese company Wanxiang bought Fisker's assets and sold the plant to developer Harvey, Hanna & Associates, which tore it down and built a logistics and fulfillment complex. "Manufacturing, if it hasn't left the country altogether, it certainly has left the state," company president Thomas J. Hanna said. The site is now an Amazon fulfillment center with three thousand employees spanning 3.7 million square feet of space.

In Quindlen's words: "Manufacturing is off the East Coast. We're the last ones that produced cars on the East Coast, and they used to be from Boston to all the way down to Doraville, Georgia. And they just don't build them anymore."

LEWES'S MENHADEN FISHERY

From the 1880s to the 1960s, oil processed from tiny fish known as menhaden grew to replace whale oil up and down the East Coast. At the center of the fishery universe was Lewes, the small coastal town at the front edge of the Delaware Bay.

A fishery needs not only boats and fishermen but also processing facilities. The first plants opened in Lewes in 1883, and the town eventually grew to land more pounds of fish than any other area in the United States. For nearly four decades, Mayor Otis Smith led both Lewes and the fishery. Menhaden went into fertilizer, vitamins and bait. Today it's an ingredient in animal feed, pet food and cosmetics.

Lewes's menhaden fisheries employed hundreds of men, both on the boats and in the processing plants. Its leader was Mayor Otis Smith. *Delaware Public Archives.*

In the industry's prime during the 1950s, more than twenty-five ships set out from Lewes to catch menhaden, crewed by hundreds of fishermen. More than 650 men labored separately in three plants to do the processing. Over half the men in Lewes worked in the fishery, hauling in more than 360 million pounds of menhaden each year; it was the largest seafood port in the country. "Lewes was a factory town," local reporter and historian Ron MacArthur wrote later. The smell permeated everything. "Even the men, all their clothes, smelled of fish," recalled one worker, Isaac Brown. Smith told his workers about the smell and odor: "What you smell was money."

By the mid-1960s, the menhaden population had declined, leading to the collapse of the fishery. Today, none of the processing plants along Cape Henlopen Drive still stand, having been replaced with beachfront houses. A net reel that was once used to dry the fishing nets, sitting on the campus of the Lewes Historical Society, is one of the few reminders of the fishery that remains today.

BUILDING SHIPS

As Delaware is a coastal state, shipbuilding was critical to its early economy. Both inland towns sitting on rivers and beachfront towns were prime building locations for ships small and large.

Lewes, sitting at the mouth of the Delaware Bay, was a hub for pilots, the commanders of two-masted schooners built in Lewes who led larger vessels up the bay toward Philadelphia's port. They were in high demand because of the shallow shoals in the area that could ground the ships carrying goods. The pilots competed against one another to reach the ships and sell their services, so speed was a key factor in their success.

But as demand rose for larger ships, Bethel—a community in western Sussex County along Broad Creek—became more prominent in Delaware's shipbuilding trade. With greater access to forests, it had natural resources that Lewes lacked. As Broad Creek is an eventual tributary of the Chesapeake Bay, a ship launched in the creek could easily access that bay and its trade via the Nanticoke River. "The town of Bethel probably owes its survival as a town to the wooden ships that were built here," one historian wrote. Bethel's "rams," as they were known, were more than one hundred feet long and took months

Top: A ship launches at Abbot's Shipyard in Milford in the 1890s. At its peak, Milford's seven shipyards employed 75 percent of city residents. *Delaware Public Archives*.

Bottom: The *Charles D. Stanford* undergoes repairs at Wilmington's Jackson & Sharp Shipyard in 1920. *Delaware Public Archives*.

to build. The first boat was built before 1835; eventually, Bethel produced thirty such ships between 1871 and 1918. Built on an incline, the ships were launched with a ship railcar, and the entire town came out to witness the event. Only a single Bethel-built ram still sails today, known as the *Victory Chimes*. Built in 1900 bearing the name *Edwin and Maud*, its home port is in Maine.

Nearby in Seaford, shipbuilding ran from 1830 to 1950, supporting commercial trade along the Nanticoke River. During World War II, the Seaford Marine Railway Co. constructed barges and boats for beach landings of troops overseas.

Stands of white oak around Milford, on the Mispillion River, made the city a shipbuilding hub in various forms from the 1780s until the 1950s. The first yard was established by the Draper family, with about twenty-two ships built by John and his son Alexander starting in 1782. The shipyards employed talented carpenters to construct the vessels; at its height, Milford was home to seven shipyards that hired three out of four city residents. The shift from wind to steam led to the industry's local decline, however. Only one survived by the 1930s, the Vinyard Shipyard, which built sub-chasers during World War I, Coast Guard boats after the war and patrol boats and more sub-chasers during World War II. After the end of the war, Vinyard switched to pleasure yachts but eventually closed down. It reopened in the 1960s, and a restoration effort is currently under way.

Milton shipbuilding began on the Broadkill River in 1737, ending in 1915. Milton was heralded for its boats for both the river and Delaware Bay, as well as hulls for other shipyards.

Wilmington, Delaware's largest city, was also the largest center of shipbuilding in the state, with about ten thousand ships turned out over the decades. Four shipbuilders operated in Wilmington, all located between the railroad and the Christina River. Harlan & Hollingsworth opened in 1836 focusing on railcar building and then ship repairs and later branched into shipbuilding. It was followed by Pusey & Jones, Jackson & Sharp and then Dravo, in the early 1900s. During World War II, Dravo became the largest concern in Wilmington, creating an assembly line process to turn out the ships. More than ten thousand people worked for the company in Wilmington. Pusey & Jones built freighters and tankers during the war, massive ships that had to be launched sideways into the Christina because they were too large to fit otherwise. But the shipyards eventually shut down and faded from modern memory. The last vessel built in Wilmington was a replica of the *Kalmar Nyckel*, the ship that brought the Swedes to Delaware in 1638, providing a fitting coda to the state's maritime heritage.

HARTMANN & FEHRENBACH BREWING COMPANY

One of Delaware's most storied breweries is the Hartmann & Fehrenbach Brewing Company, which began—as many early industries did—with a pair of immigrants. John Hartmann and John Fehrenbach were brothers-in-law hailing from Germany. They came to America in 1849 and settled in Philadelphia, where they learned the brewer's trade. Fehrenbach moved to Wilmington and opened a hotel and saloon on Fourth and French Streets. A small brewery followed at the saloon.

At Fehrenbach's urging, Hartmann joined him in Wilmington, and the duo opened up a stand-alone brewery on Lovering Avenue and Scott Street, in the Forty Acres neighborhood, in 1865. They brewed the increasingly popular lager style of beer, beginning conservatively with a one-thousand-barrel capacity. Hartmann & Fehrenbach grew steadily, selling to individuals, restaurants and hotels.

The brewery's successes underwrote an expansion of Fehrenbach's saloon in 1872. More growth soon followed. In 1878, a three-story building powered by steam boilers went up. In 1885, production hit thirty-five thousand barrels. And an 1888 expansion resulted in a four-story brewery building plus separate buildings for the engine house, wagons and stables, boilers, a cooper shop for

To stave off the tide of Prohibition, Hartmann & Fehrenbach shifted to sodas and near beer products. The new items were not enough, and it shut down in 1931. *Delaware Public Archives.*

the barrels, an ice plant and the offices—all on a three-acre site. The brewery could now turn out seventy-five thousand barrels each year.

The business soon transitioned to a new generation of German American brewers. Fehrenbach died in 1887 and Hartmann in 1890. Heirs John G. Hartmann, John G. Fehrenbach and Charles Fehrenbach took over expanding to a depot in downtown Wilmington and a bottling plant. The company was shipping to five states, and its glass bottles featured its symbol, a winged Pegasus. By 1912, it had converted from steam power to newfangled electricity.

With Prohibition looming, H&F changed its name to the Hartmann & Fehrenbach Products Company in 1919, anticipating a switch to sodas, or soft drinks, and nonalcoholic near beer. Its brands included Nu-Kola and Good Cheer, the latter with low enough alcohol content to pass muster in the days of a dry nation.

But it did not last. The company closed its doors a year later in August 1920. It remained a brewery on paper only until 1931, when it closed down. Two years later—too late for Hartmann & Fehrenbach—Prohibition ended. Few of the buildings remain. The main building was replaced by townhouses, the bottling plant is now a law office and Hartmann's saloon is now Galluccio's Restaurant and Pub.

This is just one small slice of Delaware's brewing history; a complete chronicle can be found in the book *Brewing in Delaware* by historian John Medkeff.

SUSSEX STILLS

During the Prohibition era, illegal moonshiners were most prevalent on southern Delaware's farms and remote hideaways. Raids shut down a variety of stills in Sussex County's marshes and woodlands—a fifty-gallon still in the north, four hundred gallons of mash at a farm at a place called Smokey Hollow, four stills between Lewes and Rehoboth run by teenagers, six stills and five hundred gallons of mash near Ellendale. One still near Laurel, made from a lead-lined kerosene can, was believed to have fatally poisoned a seventy-six-year-old man. Some raids sparked gunfights between the moonshiners and the agents.

The largest still in Sussex was shut down in December 1925. A few days before Christmas, a group of police raiders headed south from Georgetown to Roxana. Behind Clarence Lynch's home they found a twenty-five-gallon still and five hundred gallons of fermented mash, in barrels buried in a trench with pine slats. The Prohibition agents lined up for a commemorative photo—anticipating success, they had brought their own photographer along—and immediately after, the party was attacked by rifle fire coming from deeper into the woods. The agents beat a hasty retreat but had succeeded in ending the Roxana operation. The end of Prohibition in 1933, of course, led to the re-legalization of alcoholic consumption and the winding down of such illicit distilleries.

WAR MACHINE ON THE BRANDYWINE

The name Du Pont (or DuPont, or du Pont) has hung over Delaware like a second nickname for more than two centuries. The state's wealthiest or most prominent family, depending on which measure you use, propelled commercial investment, business and government innovation and cultural touchstones through multiple generations. (It has also been criticized for the concentration of wealth among members of a single family, the corporation's control of and influence on state and local government decisions and its conservative outlook on public affairs.)

The family's start in business in the United States came at the turn of the nineteenth century, with the founding of E.I. du Pont de Nemours & Co., in 1802. The du Ponts were French emigrants, fleeing the revolution-spackled mother country in 1800 after defending the monarchy. To start their business empire, Eleuthère Irénée du Pont purchased property for the family's powder mills from Jacob Broom on the banks of the Brandywine River, to be known as Eleutherian Mills. The du Pont enterprise promptly started churning out gunpowder, making its first sale in 1804. The company expanded in 1813 with the addition of sixty-two acres next to Eleutherian Mills called Hagley, a name that predated the du Pont ownership of the land. The Brandywine gave the powder mills their power, with the river's energy turning water wheels with the help of a millrace and dams.

Manufacturing gunpowder was not a safe occupation. In 1818, a blast known as the "Great Explosion" killed 34 people and destroyed many buildings at the complex. A year earlier, Pierre S. du Pont de Nemours died after assisting with a fire in the factory. Over 119 years, 228 people died in DuPont explosions, numbering 288.

Yet the pay was plentiful and ample, with powdermen, masons, bookkeepers, teamsters, carpenters and others often working for the firm their entire lives and using their new wealth to buy land and support their loved ones. DuPont held accounts in which employees could leave their pay and draw interest.

Powdermen earned their jobs after "considerable time at outdoor work," Alfred Victor du Pont wrote to a job applicant in the 1840s. Four men with a minimum of fifteen years of DuPont service were assigned to each of the four mills as foremen, earning one dollar a day and free housing. Du Pont family members served as superintendents, "no day going by, without our being personally in them for a number of hours."

Transporting gunpowder was also a challenge, to put it mildly, as the Hagley Museum and Library summarizes: "Shippers did not want to handle goods that could potentially kill them." Local regulations in cities such as Philadelphia caused DuPont to take an unethical and illegal approach—transporting the gunpowder in boxes labeled as other items. In the 1820s, the company halted this method, fearing that it could be found out or that an explosion might be accidentally set off.

In 1854, three wagonloads of DuPont gunpowder were being hauled through Wilmington along Fourteenth Street when they exploded. The blast of 450 kegs of powder killed the drivers, fourteen horses and two people

Working at the du Pont gunpowder mills was a dangerous business. An 1854 explosion of three wagonloads of powder in Wilmington killed the wagon drivers, two bystanders and fourteen horses. *Delaware Public Archives.*

standing nearby. Fourteenth Street was in ruins, with buildings suffering damage or complete demolition and underground water and sewer pipes wrecked. One company official theorized that a spark from a nearby factory or leaky powder kegs might have triggered the explosion. The company faced no charges and paid up to residents and businesses while assisting with the rebuilding. In response, Wilmington approved a new law banning gunpowder transport in the city limits. "The late explosion of the Messrs. Dupont's powder wagons has so shaken and terrified the city authorities that they will not allow them to pass through Wilmington any more," the *Delaware Herald* reported. In further response, DuPont built a wharf and a private road outside the city.

DuPont sold its powder to military forces around the world. During the War of 1812, it provided one million pounds of black powder to the United States, under attack from the British; the company formed its own militia in the event the Brits attacked Wilmington. DuPont also supplied the British military forces in the Crimean War in the 1850s and later provided gunpowder to the Union side during the Civil War, with a strict ban on sales to the Confederacy.

The company later branched out into dynamite production and smokeless gunpowder. After the closure of the gunpowder mills in 1921, its chemists continued creating innovation after innovation: Freon, neoprene, nylon, Teflon, Dacron, Lycra and Kevlar are all DuPont creations. Former DuPont family estates make up the Nemours children's hospital, the Winterthur museum and Longwood Gardens. The gunpowder mills are a museum and library as well, known as Hagley, standing as a testament to the power of American—and French—ingenuity and innovation.

6
MANSIONS

After standing for centuries and long decades, the homes in this chapter have crumbled, burned and been torn down through no fault of their own. In some cases, the fates of these houses ignited public interest and sparked movements for preservation, albeit too late to save them. We remember a handful of these homes here—and note that many others suffered similar ends.

SHELL HOUSE

With views of both the ocean and a lake, 2 Penn Street was perhaps the prime address in the Rehoboth Beach area for a full one hundred years.

Built by du Pont family member Margaretta Lammot du Pont Carpenter and husband Robert R. Morgan Carpenter, the mansion known as Shell House was just south of Rehoboth proper. It sat in county land squeezed between Rehoboth and Dewey Beach. Money was no object for the family: Margaretta's great-grandfather founded the DuPont Co., and Robert was an owner of the Phillies.

Shell House, used as a summer beach house, stayed in the du Pont Carpenter family for eighty-seven years. Other Carpenters built cottages on neighboring properties. The home gained later particular fame as the warm-weather home of Louisa D'Andelot Carpenter, daughter of Margaretta and Robert, and served as a spark for Rehoboth Beach's LGBTQ community.

Relatively out for the time, no doubt assisted by her family's fortunes, Louisa was an accomplished equestrian, hunter and pilot and was known for wearing men's clothing. Her partners over the years included singer Libby Holman and possibly Eugenia Bankhead, and she partied with celebrities like Tallulah Bankhead, Greta Garbo and Noël Coward at Shell House.

After Holman was accused of murdering her husband, Carpenter paid her bail; when the charges were dropped, they came to Delaware together. After Holman's suicide in 1971, Louisa continued an avid social life at Shell House. She died in a plane crash flying to Easton in 1976, at age sixty-eight.

In 2007, Margaretta Lammot du Pont Carpenter's grandchildren sold Shell House to an almost equally distinguished scion, Meredith Townsend. Her grandfather John G. Townsend Jr. was a former Delaware governor and two-term U.S. senator and built chicken company Townsends Inc.

Townsend held on to it until 2019, when it became the priciest house on the market in Delaware at that time, listing for $14.9 million. That was only the second time Shell House had been on the open market.

The once-proud Shell House, just south of the Rehoboth Beach city limits, was demolished in 2020. *Courtesy of the* Cape Gazette, *photo by Chris Flood.*

Townsend did a complete overhaul and restoration of the house and expanded it to 7,800 square feet. The 2019 listing boasted of modern amenities (Sub-Zero refrigerators, six-burner gas range, two ovens) combined with 1920s charm (antique tile floors, exposed beams, red cedar shake siding).

Yet the house's location, fame and history were not enough. The property went unsold, and in August 2020, heavy equipment moved in and the home was demolished. The two lots it sat on were then put up for sale individually—potentially worth more as buildable land than for the historic home's value.

LAWRENCE

Built around 1840, Lawrence was a tall white house with a four-column front, echoing the Greek Revival style. It was constructed for Charles Wright, a businessman and shipper, who had the mansion built for his second wife, Eliza Ann Mastin, after they married in 1839.

The "temple front" style was "unusual for Delaware, even for public buildings," historians noted in a 1977 report for the National Register of Historic Places. "Few temple fronts were built and fewer survive." They observed that the design was likely not the work of a local architect: "This building radically departs in nearly every detail from the vernacular architecture then prevalent in the area."

The nearly 50-year-old survey reveals that Lawrence was a survivor. The house, around 130 years old then, was mostly intact and preserved from its earliest days; the exterior, porches, shutters, mantels and trim were all original. Of special note were the locks—"an inventory of the finest materials available during the period," including carpenter-type latches, iron rimblocks and mortise locks. "Lawrence is a nearly-complete surviving example of the classic period in American domestic architecture," the report's authors concluded.

The property located on US 13-A outside Seaford was then owned by Mr. and Mrs. Dallas Culver. Mr. Culver was president of a fertilizer manufacturer, county jury commissioner, a director of the former Sussex Trust bank and a three-time member of the State Highway Commission.

Yet by the mid-2000s, it stood in shambles, empty and abandoned and on the verge of demolition. Alerted too late, local preservationists rallied to

Pictured in 1969, Lawrence became a symbol for historical preservation advocates in Delaware and especially in Sussex County after its demolition. *Delaware Public Archives.*

the cause but were unsuccessful. Sussex County had no historic preservation statute in place to even document privately owned buildings before they were torn down. "Lawrence was one of a kind. There's no other house like it in this entire state," reflected Dan Parsons, Sussex County's historic planner.

The death of Lawrence spurred many to act to keep other houses from being demolished. Efforts to preserve the Cannon-Maston House, also outside of Seaford on Atlanta Road, later succeeded, with the county government and a local land trust joining forces.

"The only way we can be sure that somebody doesn't destroy it is to own it," said Anne Nesbit, a historic preservation advocate from Seaford.

GHOSTS OF CANNON HALL

Say the name Cannon in Sussex County, and what comes most frequently to mind is the murderer and kidnapper Patty Cannon, known for her gang's reign of terror in both Delaware and Maryland.

Cannon Hall was built by another Cannon entirely. Jacob Cannon was a businessman, merchant and prominent landowner in western Sussex County; the enslaving family once owned more than 4,500 acres. Local legend holds that he built the home for his fiancée, who dumped him, and that it sat unoccupied for decades. Jacob and his brother Isaac reportedly made many enemies as their wealth grew, including as a result of foreclosures. A state historian once characterized Jacob as "a bitter, lonely man" notable for his "fabled miserliness"; a 1930s historian declared of Jacob that "money was his God."

The wood-frame house was built around 1812–20. Architectural historian W. Barksdale Maynard reports that it reflects the style of the Tidewater regions of Virginia and Maryland with its brick foundation and layout. It included five working chimneys.

It was later occupied by Jacob and Isaac's sister Luraney Boling and her daughter, Julia Ann Hall, who both contributed to the building of local churches in Woodland. When a fire once consumed the first church and winds threatened Cannon Hall, Hall reportedly prayed for the protection of the home. She financed the building of a new church and opened the home to the Methodist congregation until it was finished in 1883.

Later lore says the house was haunted by the ghost of Boling or Hall. The Griffies family, who saw and felt the ghost, reported they had come to an agreement not to disturb her, planning no renovations or seances. "If she wants to stay here, fine," said Jeff Griffies. "She is welcome and I guess we are welcome. If not, we'd be gone." Former owner Marilee Bradley recalled that she never saw ghosts. "Once in a great while my bed would tremble," she said. "But I have no idea. It didn't scare me."

Marilee and Fulton Bradley purchased the home in 1961 and worked to restore it for the next eleven years. Fulton, who died in 1981, aimed for original materials or brought in items from the same period. The living room floor was redone with wood from a Crisfield, Maryland schoolhouse, using wooden pegs. They finally moved in on their thirtieth anniversary, in 1972.

Cannon Hall burned in a fire in 2010. It apparently started in the dining room area due to an electrical issue while the then owner, Marilyn Griffies, was thankfully in her barn with her dogs at the time. Efforts were under way to rebuild.

The home is located in the hamlet of Woodland, outside Seaford, which was formerly called Cannon's Ferry after the river-crossing vessel that the

Located in the hamlet of Woodland, across from the eponymous ferry, Cannon Hall was built in the 1810s and is purportedly haunted. *Delaware Public Archives.*

Cannon family used to operate there. It was started by Jacob Cannon's grandfather James Cannon around 1740. Now known as the Woodland Ferry, the cable-guided boat still operates today taking passengers and cars across the Nanticoke River, run by the Delaware Department of Transportation. Cannon Hall sits opposite the ferry across Woodland Church Road on the Seaford side of the river.

Jacob Cannon died in 1843, shot on the ferry landing across from Cannon Hall after accusing another man of stealing a gum tree that held a precious beehive. Legend says that about fifty people witnessed the murder and let the gunman escape, a testament to the depth of dislike for Cannon.

WOODLAWN

It's hard to imagine a house described as "plucky," but the enduring qualities of Woodlawn made it so. Built for a prosperous Smyrna-area merchant in the 1730s–40s, the estate of Woodlawn was, at the time of its demise, notable for its status as the last remaining Greek Revival home in Delaware. Its landmark white columns standing along US 13 were another symbol of the state's vanished past fallen to developers' heavy equipment.

The building had been a home, a candy store and a restaurant. It was rumored to have been haunted and an Underground Railroad stop. And along the way, vicious and unfounded calumnies against one woman owner claimed it had been a brothel.

Woodlawn was also known as the Thomas England House for the property's original owner, though England possessed it for only two years and never lived in the house. It was given to him in 1709 by William Penn and sold to James Morris in 1711, who built the original house. A Greek Revival front was added in 1853 by G.W. Cummins, one of the wealthiest men in Kent County, whose holdings spanned 2,500 acres. Cummins's father was a merchant who shipped goods from Wilmington and Philadelphia by boat and wagons, and he made his wealth much the same way.

Historians who surveyed the property prior to its National Register nomination in 1981 surmised that it was built as a log house, expanded to a two-floor home with a framed second story, expanded with a two-story addition of brick and then deepened and the Greek Revival front put on. The original exterior walls were three bricks wide and the interior walls two bricks wide, all brought over from Europe.

"It is remarkable that the house in its final state possesses the interior unity that it does," wrote historian Patricia Wright, noting that the "plucky resolution of the special problems of re-use" made Woodlawn "peculiarly and satisfyingly Delawarean."

Robert Fagan Sr. owned it from the 1970s to the late 1980s as a restaurant. It was then purchased by George "Dusty" Rhoads, who owned it and ran the restaurant until his death in 2012. The town had discussed annexing the house over the years, but nothing came of it. Vacant for several years, it was purchased by a company called Liborio III LLC, which made plans to tear it down. That happened in 2017.

"When they tore down the back of it, the original part, I kind of cried the whole night," said Charles Woodley III, who lived across US 13. County

Shown in 1926, Woodlawn in Smyrna was built for merchant G.W. Cummins, one of Kent County's wealthiest men. *Delaware Public Archives.*

Commissioner Brooks Banta echoed that sentiment. "It's a horrible thing to do without at least consulting with people in the area who have patronized the house and made memories in it over the years," he said.

Marisa Reeder, whose grandfather was Robert Fagan, remembered playing in the cornfields and her cousins working in the restaurant. "It made us sad and frustrated that such a beautiful building was allowed to degrade over time like that, but now it's gone. You cannot replace history like that," she said.

THE HERMITAGE

The Hermitage, an Old New Castle landmark, was most notable for its ownership by U.S. Senator Nicholas Van Dyke. An attorney and graduate of what would become Princeton University, he served in the Delaware House of Representatives starting in 1799 until joining the US Senate in 1816.

The Hermitage was built in several phases between 1801 and 1818 by U.S. Senator Nicholas Van Dyke. It burned in a 2007 arson. *Delaware Public Archives.*

Originally purchased by Van Dyke from the Finney family for use as a farm and summer retreat in 1799, it was then 141 acres of the original 190. The house was built in stages from 1801 to 1818. It was a two-story brick structure composed of thirty-one rooms, including seven bedrooms, five baths and two and a half kitchens. The west wing is believed to have been the oldest area. The north area held a kitchen and pantry with lodging for servants above, and the south or main section was built last, in 1818, featuring a widow's walk on the roof.

In 1949, the property was sold by descendants of the Van Dyke family to the Deemers, who planned to do renovations and live in the home. "The imposing old structure is a commanding sight along the main route of ferry travel," a Wilmington newspaper noted. By the 1970s, the rest of the land had been sold off and only the home remained. It was often open during A Day in Old New Castle festivities for tours.

But one cold night in February 2007, the home was struck by arson, causing $1 million damage. Thousands of dollars in antiques were destroyed by the blaze, which took nine fire companies six hours to get under control. The Hermitage would stand no more.

7
MEDICINE

The practice of medicine in Delaware is currently big business. Our hospitals employ more than 22,000 Delawareans and see more than 376,000 ER visits and 85,000 admissions each year. But healthcare began in a rudimentary fashion, with town doctors or police officers binding up wounds and patients largely recovering at their own homes. The stories of the hospitals in this chapter help piece together and reconstruct the larger story of Delaware medicine.

TILTON GENERAL HOSPITAL

Tilton General Hospital was one of two hundred military hospitals operated by the Union during the Civil War. Open for two years in Wilmington, it accommodated 350 patients (more if tents were set up in the courtyard). Doctors, surgeons and convalescent patients cared for the sick and wounded patients; there were no female nurses at that time.

Tilton patients included Cyrus Forwood, a farmer from Brandywine Hundred who served with the Second Delaware Regiment. Wounded in the thigh at the Battle of Gettysburg, Forwood was sent to Tilton Hospital by rail car.

Yet Tilton's relatively short history belies the impact of its namesake—the Delaware physician who was the first surgeon general of the United States.

A Civil War hospital in Wilmington, Tilton Hospital was open for only two years. It was named after James Tilton, the first U.S. surgeon general. *Delaware Public Archives.*

James Tilton was a Revolutionary War patriot, army officer and physician, born in Kent County and a graduate of the College of Philadelphia, later the University of Pennsylvania. He led hospitals in New Jersey and New York and was a critic of poor ventilation and unsanitary conditions that spread disease.

Tilton's post–Revolutionary War career was spent in private practice back in Dover, serving in the Continental Congress and as a member of the state House, as well as state commissioner of loans. He later moved his medical practice and farm to the Wilmington area and in 1813 published a book on military hospitals dedicated to the then secretary of war. In March of that year, with the War of 1812 underway, Tilton was named chief physician and surgeon general of the army, confirmed by the Senate in June.

Tilton focused his work on inspecting the military hospitals at the northern edge of the United States, where he found poor sanitation and neglect in care. He moved hospitals, created new ones and shifted poor medical staff out. A year later, Tilton published regulations outlining the exact duties of the medical staff—the first time they had been established.

Other hospitals would be named after Tilton, including an army hospital at Fort Dix in New Jersey. His home in Wilmington is now the University and Whist Club, and Tilton Park in the city is named in his honor.

A CITY OF THREE HOSPITALS

The story of Wilmington's hospitals begins with a medical battle royale. The 1800s was a time of change and of competing styles of healthcare, between homeopaths and allopaths. The two schools of thought differed in their approach to treating disease. The homeopaths gave patients small doses of cures that would create symptoms of the disease in a healthy person; the allopaths created a reaction in the patient that fought the disease.

In the late 1800s, injuries were typically treated at doctor's offices or the police station. Railroad accidents were handled by the Wilmington railroad detective, who was also the town surgeon. If there were amputations, the patient was sent home to recover. There were no formal operating rooms and women gave birth at home. It was clear to many that Wilmington needed a hospital—but the two schools of medicine refused to share a building and work together.

Delaware's Homeopathic Hospital began in the former Heald Home at Van Buren Street and Shallcross Avenue. It later became part of ChristianaCare. *Delaware Public Archives.*

The first hospital was founded in 1888 by the homeopaths, dubbed the Homeopathic Hospital. It was opened in a former private hospital called the Hygeian Home, at Van Buren Street and Shallcross Avenue. The doctors provided care to anyone without reference to race, gender, age or religion. There were no limitations on financial status—the hospital took all patients without considering their ability to pay. There were 271 patients treated the first year. In 1940, it was renamed Memorial Hospital—and, in a sign that the allopaths had won, began offering both styles of care.

The allopaths formed their venture a few years later, in 1890 at Fourteenth and Washington Streets. Called Delaware Hospital, it treated 161 people in the first year. Quickly added on were private rooms, an X-ray department, a children's ward, a mother's milk bank for premature babies and a maternity floor. By 1939, Delaware Hospital saw five thousand patients each year. Three additional buildings came online before 1942, and in 1981, it was renovated for $22 million.

A third hospital opened in 1910, the Physicians and Surgeons Hospital at Eighth and Adams Streets, in the former William Bowe mansion. It had twenty-eight beds to start but over the decades added a contagious disease unit, a training school, a nurses' residence and a maternity ward, all by 1938. Private labor and delivery rooms came after 1965. Eventually, its name was changed to the Wilmington General Hospital Association—or Wilmington General for short.

The three hospitals could not stand apart forever. In 1965, they merged, and each became a separate "division" of the umbrella Wilmington Medical Center. But rapid growth in the 1970s, combined with increasing maintenance and physical plant issues, forced additional changes. The hospital's "Plan Omega" called for an entirely new hospital to be built outside the city, near Christiana. The Memorial Hospital building (formerly the Homeopathic Hospital) and Wilmington General were torn down and the properties razed. ChristianaCare opened in 1985 and is now the state's largest healthcare system.

EMILY BISSELL HOSPITAL

Wilmington social activist Emily Bissell was known for her efforts to help Delawareans stricken by tuberculosis, an infectious lung disease that was once the leading cause of death in the United States. At the time, the only treatment available for patients with tuberculosis—also called "consumption"—was rest and fresh air.

Bissell's cousin Dr. Joseph Wales ran an open-air convalescent hospital for TB called the Brandywine Sanatorium or the "Brandywine Shack." In 1907, he wrote to Emily asking for help in raising $300 to keep the sanatorium going through the winter. Inspired by a program in Denmark, Bissell designed a "Christmas seal," a fancy stamp that could be affixed to Christmas cards and sold them from a table in the Wilmington post office. With advertising help from a Philadelphia newspaper and the endorsement of President Theodore Roosevelt, instead of $300, Bissell raised $3,000. In 1908, Bissell's friend and well-known illustrator Howard Pyle designed the second seal.

The ongoing success of Bissell's Christmas Seals allowed the sanatorium to expand, acquiring a property west of Wilmington along what is today known as Newport Gap Pike. By September 1909, the sanatorium was full, with a twenty-person waitlist.

The property was known as Hope Farm and the Brandywine Sanitorium until the 1950s, when it was renamed for Bissell, who died in 1948 after spending years as president of the Delaware Anti-Tuberculosis Society. The sanatorium expanded over the years, serving 125 patients in 1959.

Better hygiene practices and public health efforts to educate Americans on how to avoid and treat tuberculosis caused cases of the disease to decline in the 1920s and 1930s. In the 1940s and 1950s, drugs were developed that could effectively treat tuberculosis, causing a significant drop in the need for facilities like the Bissell Hospital. There were 84,304 cases of TB in the United States in 1953; by 1959, the number of cases had dropped to 57,535.

In 1957, the facility was renamed Emily P. Bissell Hospital, to reflect that patients "are being given modern, intensive hospital treatment; drug therapy, surgery and rehabilitation. The word 'sanatorium' implies that only rest, food, fresh air and natural therapeutic agents are used in treating patients," according to a *News Journal* article about the change.

The need for tuberculosis treatment continued to decline, and the State of Delaware converted Bissell into a long-term care facility for low-income elderly patients in 1975. Almost right away, reports began to circulate in the media about poor care for the patients who lived there. Longtime *News Journal* columnist Bill Frank called the Bissell Hospital a "disgrace to the state of Delaware" in 1976, and a 1979 article noted that

The Emily Bissell Hospital, named in honor of the creator of Christmas Seals, was open from the early 1900s until 2015. *Delaware Public Archives.*

"hopelessness hangs in the air" of the hospital, "thick and inescapable as the odors of incontinence."

But over the next three decades, little was done to improve conditions at Bissell. In 2008, two sisters used a hidden camera to expose the poor treatment of their aunt, a resident there. Their videos showed physical and emotional abuse of patients by employees. The exposure of the videos caused three employees to be fired and two to be suspended. The facility continued to operate until 2015, when a temporary closure to fix the hot water system became permanent. At the time, fewer than fifty patients were living at Bissell.

The hospital building and other structures on the property currently sit abandoned, empty, covered with graffiti and obscured by overgrown weeds, trees and other debris. The State of Delaware has sought bids for a new use for the property, but officials say it will likely take years for any new development to come to fruition.

8
PUBLIC LIFE

It's fitting to begin this chapter with a lost language of an ancient people still here today—the Nanticoke. The other stories here cover governmental institutions, communities and their spirit and public service. We know that many stories that haven't lasted until now are merely hidden from view; bringing them to light is the only way to keep traditions and heritage alive.

THE NANTICOKE LANGUAGE

The Nanticokes are Delaware's First Peoples—here before William Penn's "Lower Counties," here before the Swedes landed at Fort Christina, here before the Dutch settled Zwaanendael and here before John Smith sailed to the mouth of Broad Creek.

The tribe is still here today, small in numbers but strong in spirit and proud of its heritage. Its cultural and physical history is centered in Sussex County, around Millsboro, Oak Orchard and Riverdale. The tribe won state recognition in 1903, and the modern-day Nanticoke Indian Association formed in 1922.

What's become lost over the decades, though, is the language that once bound the people together. The last native speaker of the Nanticoke language died in 1856, in her seventies or eighties. Lydia H. Clark's descendants would go on to lead the tribe in later generations; what was believed to be her grave was rediscovered in the 1930s.

But only fragments of her language remain: a 1785 list of words by a missionary, a 1792 list from a Maryland congressman—and some glossaries conflict.

Work has been underway in various forms to reconstruct the vanished tongue. In the mid-2000s, a Canadian teacher of the Anishnabay language traveled to Delaware to lead lessons in Nanticoke, leaving behind audio recordings to help more tribal members to learn.

"A lot of tribes don't understand how you can survive without a language," said the late Nanticoke chief James T. "Tee" Norwood. "It's a certain bond that you have. It just connects you more."

More recently, a group of tribal members, anthropologists and linguists have pieced together vocabulary from those centuries-old dictionaries and added in borrowed words and phrases from sister languages from other tribes. They have produced a book and are working toward other resources, workbooks and games.

"The Algonquian languages of the Eastern Seaboard are related and similar to each other, so we are all able to lean on each other as we work on language revitalization," said Karelle Hall, a Nanticoke tribal member and doctoral student in anthropology at Rutgers.

Counting to five in Nanticoke is *nukwit*, *nils*, *nuhsw*, *yaaw* and *nupayaa*. You would say *Waanishii* instead of "thank you."

As for Lydia Clark, her name was Nau-Gwa-Ok-Wa. It means "She Who Bows Her Head in Prayer."

CHENEY CLOW'S FORT

The American Revolution's battles largely swirled around outside of Delaware, with a handful of exceptions. One such incident took place in Kent County in 1778, with many "facts" surrounding it being the product of local myth and legend rather than history. State historical records and reputable historians generally appear to agree on the following details.

The "rebellion" began with a British-born Tory-allied landowner named Cheney (or Cheyney) Clow, described as a "local eccentric." He refused to pay his taxes to Delaware, claiming that he was a resident of Maryland.

Clow's home was about six hundred feet on the Delaware side of the border, which had been established several years prior.

At some point, Clow was able to obtain a commission of unclear rank in the British army and began organizing a Loyalist militia, which then raided their neighbors' farms and holdings. Numbering about 150, Clow's men built a log fort in a swampy area near Gravelly Branch.

In April 1778, a colonial militia commander, Lieutenant Colonel Charles Pope, arrived in the area after entreaties from the local residents, tired of being terrorized by Clow and his confederates. Pope's fighting force camped at a place called Grogtown, now known as Kenton, and he summoned reinforcements. They raided Clow's fort and burned it, but the leader of the Loyalist insurgency fled. (Left behind were "about a thousand weight of bacon and two barrels of flower which they stole," contemporary records reported.)

Former president of Delaware Caesar Rodney wrote of his concern that Clow's movement could have sparked more Loyalist sentiment: "They increased verry [*sic*] fast and I believe, if they had not been opposed very suddenly and with Spirit, they would have become formidable in a Little time."

A month later, the state assembly required a loyalty oath to the Revolution, which Clow refused to take. In 1782, Clow was arrested and charged with treason. During the arrest, he and his wife fought back by firing on the sheriff. Clad in his British uniform, Clow was taken back to Dover for trial. Acquitted of treason, he was eventually tried and sentenced to death by hanging for murder but was not executed until 1788. It was reported that after his death, Clow became a popular symbol of a political martyr who had been unfairly executed. It is not known where his wife buried his body.

The precise location of Clow's fort is not known today. It is believed to have been located on two properties, one of which was owned by a Patriot family. Archaeological surveys done as of the 1970s failed to turn up evidence of the site. Decades later, some of the burned logs were still reported to be visible in the swamps, but today the marshes have likely covered the site. "It is unlikely that many surface indications would be found in the plowed fields nearby," state historians glumly reported.

One local farmer, whose family had owned one of the properties since the 1930s, recalled in the 1990s finding a burned area during an excavation, about fifteen feet square. He recalled people digging on the land in search of money that Clow had reportedly hidden to finance a British raid up the Chesapeake Bay. "I used to dig around, too, but never did find anything," Joseph G. Ford told a reporter.

DELAWARE'S POW CAMPS

It has been about eight decades since the end of World War II, and largely forgotten in that time span is the existence of prisoner-of-war camps on Delaware soil. There are few reminders remaining today, but for a few years during the titanic struggle against the Axis, POWs helped with some of the First State's most pressing problems of manpower on the homefront.

The prisoners—from Germany, Austria and Italy—were processed and initially held at Fort DuPont, near Delaware City. From 1942 to 1946, the fort held up to 3,000 POWs, including the crew of the German U-boat that surrendered off Fort Miles, at Cape Henlopen. During the course of the war, more than 400,000 German and Italian prisoners were held in the United States.

Satellite camps were set up around the state, at Lewes, Slaughter Beach, Georgetown, Harbeson and what is now the state fairgrounds in

German prisoners of war on a work detail at Fort DuPont. POWs helped bring in crops from satellite camps across Kent and Sussex Counties. *Delaware Public Archives.*

Harrington. Fort Saulsbury, at Slaughter Beach, held about one thousand Germans and Italians.

With 33,000 Delaware men serving overseas in the armed forces, workers were needed to bring in crops, run canning machines, labor at lumber mills and work in kitchens. Farms were especially in need of help at harvest time, short of 3,500 men. The work was voluntary and under the Geneva Conventions. POWs would work a maximum of six twelve-hour days a week and earned ninety cents an hour. At canneries in Wyoming and Houston there were 400 workers alone; 550 from Austria would step into roles in a chicken processing plant while living at the fairgrounds—often producing enough extra chicken to feed both the POWs and their GI guards.

Later a U.S. Army major, Second Lieutenant George Kates was assigned to the Georgetown camp and later led the building of the Harrington sub-camp. Kates wrote that he had "unlimited credit in any store in Harrington for any supplies or equipment needed and no questions asked."

Prisoners also were assigned to the Dover Army Airfield, doing KP and housekeeping—duties that airmen were too valuable to spend time doing. The POWs were lightly guarded and prohibited from fraternization. There were a few escape attempts, including a desperate leap from a truck going to a chicken plant in Millsboro; the four men were back in custody within a few hours.

By war's end, more than 6,500 German and Austrian prisoners had come through Delaware. They stuck around even after the Nazi defeat in 1945; their repatriation date was delayed several months into 1946 to meet additional labor challenges.

There are few reminders today of the Axis POWs and their service to the state. One such tangible monument, standing as of the 2020s, is a chicken house that prisoners built amid the peach and apple orchards of T.S. Smith & Sons in Bridgeville. It featured a caretakers' cottage on top.

THE PRISON AT PRICES CORNER

The prison at Prices Corner began with a quaint if Dickensian name, the New Castle County Workhouse Women's Ward. It was designed to alleviate crowding at another prison, the New Castle County Workhouse in what is now Greenbank Park. The new facility was built with inmate labor and opened in 1929.

Founded as a women's correctional facility, the prison building at Prices Corner later housed men. It was named after John Webb, Delaware's first Black warden. *Courtesy of the Delaware Department of Correction.*

The three-story prison's design was cutting-edge for its time. The women incarcerated there lived in dorm-style accommodations rather than cells. There were classes in cooking, typing and sewing; outdoor space for exercise and fresh air; and gardens to grow plants. Inmates were permitted to decorate their living areas with curtains, and the solitary cell known as "the hole" featured walls with butterflies. Each room had a bell that could alert matrons to emergencies.

The sixty inmates had been sentenced there for crimes ranging from bootlegging to murder, truly spanning the gamut of criminal offenses. Over the years, the prisoners included Margaret H. Fisher, who killed her husband by poisoning his soup with cyanide and arsenic. Sentenced to life in 1961, she was oddly employed as a cook in the prison kitchen.

In the 1970s, it became co-ed, as eight men joined twenty-one women. In 1975, the women were moved to a former school in Claymont, and the Prices Corner location became a pre-trial site just holding men. In 1994, it was renamed the John L. Webb Correctional Facility, after Delaware's first Black warden. Webb had served as an officer and then warden of the pre-trial annex. The prison was closed in 2016, with state officials citing the lack of physical accessibility for people with disabilities and the expensive maintenance. It was later used as a training site for correctional officers.

In recent years, the empty prison was demolished to make room for a new state police troop complex. The prison site would be used for evidence storage and vehicle maintenance. Preservationists tried to save the building but were unsuccessful.

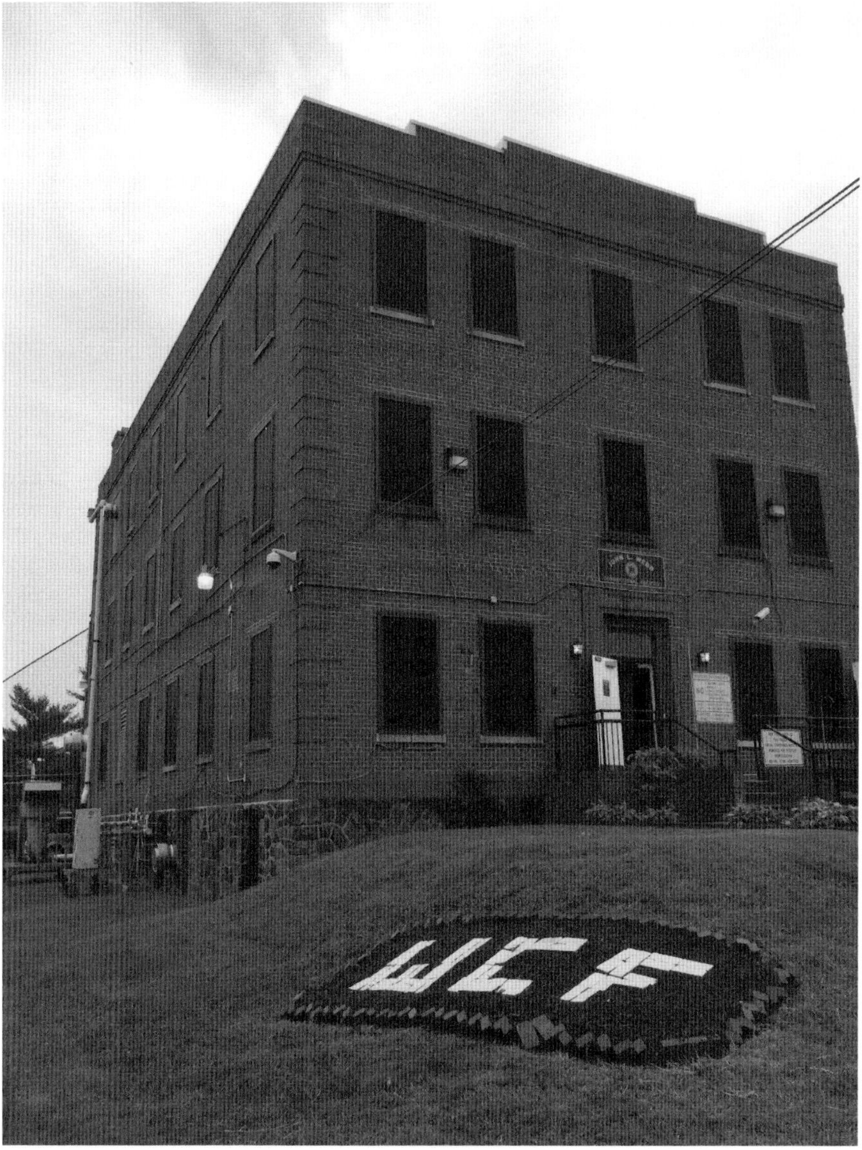

The prison building was closed in 2016 and later demolished to make room for a state police complex. *Courtesy of the Delaware Department of Correction.*

"It was a creepy building," recalled Corie Priest, who had been incarcerated there and later worked as a community engagement specialist with the state Department of Justice. "But they kind of made it work for us."

THE WHIPPING POST

Law and order versus barbarism and racism. That was the dichotomy for years represented by Delaware's whipping posts. The First State was the final state to abolish whipping as criminal punishment and, in a final coda, only removed the final whipping post from public display under pressure in 2020.

It took the national reflection sparked by the police murder of George Floyd that summer to yank the post from a museum's grounds and place it in storage. The state's plans for the post include the possibility of a museum display, developed with local Black leaders and educators, where it could be featured with historical context. (As of this writing, the state is working on a plan but has not announced it publicly.)

Back in the whipping post's heyday, however, it was praised as a form of punishment—and also functioned as public entertainment of sorts. The writer Theodore Dreiser visited Delaware in 1900 to write an article on the practice, citing favorably the discipline espoused by Cotton Mather and John Winthrop in colonial times. Dreiser watched a crowd of about two hundred people watch the lashings outside the Delaware Street courthouse in New Castle—laughing, wincing, smiling and watching with eyes wide.

The whipping post's use as a tool of racist enforcement was openly spoken of. About 70 to 90 percent of those punished were Black men, Dreiser and his sources estimated. "It is the only way we have of reaching them," a sheriff told Dreiser—referring to Black men. (A later study examining the years from 1900 to 1945 found that 67 percent of the people whipped were Black, who at the time comprised less than a fifth of Delaware's population.)

One account of a whipping comes from Dr. Reba Hollingsworth, vice-chair of the Delaware Heritage Commission when the post was removed. She recalled watching a late 1930s whipping at the Kent County jail in Dover: "I still remember the eerie silence that was pierced by the lashes of the whip. After each lash, the warden would loudly count each lash."

Judges imposed whipping as a sentence to punish a variety of offenses, from theft to rape, with twenty-one crimes in total eligible for the lash. These included poisoning with intent to murder; burning a courthouse; burglary with explosives at night (though apparently not during the day); stealing a horse, ass or mule by breaking a lock; embezzlement; dangerously obstructing railroad tracks; perjury; or putting up fake lights to wreck a ship.

In the 1850s, a limit of sixty lashes at a time was imposed; the laws were later relaxed to exempt children, white women and Black women from the punishment, the latter change occurring in 1889.

Delaware's whipping post in Georgetown was finally removed in 2020. Plans are underway for an appropriate explanatory exhibit. *Courtesy of the Delaware Division of Historic and Cultural Affairs.*

Eventually, as society became less tolerant of corporal punishment, Delaware became a laughingstock of the nation for the persistence of the practice. Lawmakers eventually barred cameras from whippings, hoping to clamp down on the ridicule; having a camera near the scene could result in a $1,000 fine or six months in prison.

The last whipping in Delaware was conducted in 1952, and whipping was abolished as a punishment by the enlightened days of 1972. It was the last state in the union to do so.

The posts were removed one by one from the state prison grounds in the 1970s, except for the pillar at the prison south of Georgetown. In 1992, the warden donated it to the state's historic affairs agency. It was installed in the county seat in 1993, secured into the lawn of the Old Sussex County Courthouse, now a historic site, behind a small railing.

But by the summer of 2020, its days were over. Jackhammered out of the ground, the eight-foot post was removed on July 1 and hauled north to Dover to a state storage facility. It would sit there along with Dover's former whipping post.

Hollingsworth was a supporter of eventually placing the post in a museum, with proper displays to interpret and explain the era from whence it came. "I don't want them destroyed, personally. I think if you destroy the past then the future doesn't really understand the past," she said. "But I don't think that we need to actually view them every time we pass through Georgetown, or Dover, or New Castle."

There in Georgetown watching the removal was Valarie Dacius of Seaford, with her six-year-old son. "It's important for us to stand against things that have been symbols of hate," she said. "It's important for bigger changes. It's important for him to see this."

Postscript: A final part of the story is about the actual whips used to administer the lashes. The state Division of Historical and Cultural Affairs believes there are five—one in a private home in Dover and four in the state's collections, two of which are in a wooden and glass case.

GLENVILLE

The neighborhood of Glenville—a community of nearly two hundred ranch homes, featuring plenty of room for growing families, with four bedrooms and basements—was born during the heyday of the Cold War. The houses sold for $12,500 in 1959 or about $128,000 today.

But over the decades, Glenville became known mostly for its susceptibility to flooding in severe weather. It was hit hard by Floyd in 1999 and then slammed by the remnants of Tropical Storm Henri in 2003.

Over three days that September, up to ten inches of rain had lashed the northern part of the state. Flash floods washed out entire roads—plus much of the structure of the Wooddale covered bridge. The Red Clay Creek surged.

Emergency responders went into action, with helicopters and boats coming to the rescue of stranded residents and drivers. Evacuations in Glenville drew the National Guard, New Castle County police and twenty to thirty other first responder agencies from around the region that offered their marine rescue units. Fifty people were ultimately evacuated. One of Delaware's best reporters, Beth Miller of the *News Journal*, who would cover the community's saga for several more years, summed up the scene at an evacuation point: "Many arrived at the intersection with pets, a few had packed bags, and some had a few things thrown into plastic grocery bags. Some were sobbing. Some had called for help while others left their homes only under threat of arrest."

As the floodwaters receded, leaders were taking steps to keep it from happening again. A state task force supported a buyout plan by November, and appraisals began a month later. The government moved quickly, with the county contributing $15 million and the Delaware Department of Transportation settling on the first 5 homes by April 2004. A year after the Henri flooding, 110 homes were purchased, with other buyouts pending. The project cost $33 million total, including $23 million for home deals and relocation aid.

"People who really did not trust each other were able to put it all aside for this project," said then county executive Chris Coons (now a U.S. senator). "There were a dozen times it could have fallen through."

By August 2005, with deals signed and residents gone, the Glenville demolition began. Four families still lived in condemned homes, holding out for more, and the deal left twenty homes still standing because they were not in a flood zone. But many houses had been vandalized and hit with graffiti. Some had to have environmental remediation work done, such as asbestos removal, before the heavy equipment could go to work.

But not everyone was happy. One couple who demolished their home after Floyd spent $250,000 to rebuild and were offered $309,900 for the buyout and expenses.

The Wooddale Bridge, spanning the Red Clay Creek, was wrecked in 2003 by Tropical Storm Henri. It was rebuilt and reopened five years later. *Delaware Public Archives.*

Mallette Greenwood Conley grew up in Glenville and was one of a handful of former residents who returned for a sort of demolition watch party. "It was kind of sad to be there, but not really," she said. "Long after Glenville's gone, we'll still have those friendships and memories."

LAUREL'S LEWIS MURAL

Jack Lewis was perhaps Delaware's most famous popular public artist. Known for his unique style and large murals, he honed his skills with the Civilian Conservation Corps during the 1930s. He moved to Bridgeville, taught art in public schools and at Delaware Technical Community College and published several books of artwork. He also served with the U.S. Army Corps of Engineers in the Pacific theater during World War II.

Jack Lewis at his artist's desk in 1940. Lewis adopted Sussex County as his home, residing in Bridgeville for many years. *Delaware Public Archives.*

In 1993, he and a team of volunteers brought their talents to Laurel, crafting a mural on the side of the Laurel Senior Center's gift shop. It featured highlights of Laurel's past, including the Woodland Ferry, Old Christ Church, Broad Creek and Rosemont Mansion. The ten-part mural was created after three abandoned buildings that covered up the wall were demolished as part of the town's redevelopment. The mural was modeled after a similar one on the side of a store in Bridgeville that Lewis had painted in 1992.

Lewis was eighty years old at the time but climbed up on scaffolding and reached out to paint the scenes like he was in his thirties. He hoped the mural would lend an artistic element to Laurel's downtown. "As these little towns are left high and dry, there's an increasing effort to bring people back to them with such charming elements as a mural," Lewis told a reporter.

Just four years later, the mural was threatened with demolition. Utilities and insurance costs plus a new roof and painting inside were estimated at over $10,000, and the thrift shop had closed in the meantime. The senior center wanted to tear the building down for a parking lot so clients with disabilities could be dropped off more easily for their day programs. "We need some space and nobody is listening to us," director Penny Duncan said. "They're just concerned about a building. My concern, on the other hand, is about people."

Residents—and Lewis—protested, with about twenty people forming a human chain on the day of the scheduled demolition, and the work was paused. "We don't need another vacant lot down here," said Richard L. Stone, the newly elected mayor. "If we could have the building and somebody occupying it, it's going to get people downtown, and that's what we are after."

The senior center planned to donate it to the local Boys & Girls Club. But ultimately, the building had to be demolished, and Lewis's mural went with it. Lewis died at age ninety-nine, a few days short of one hundred. His works can be seen today in Legislative Hall, in the Bridgeville Public Library and at Delaware Tech's Owens Campus in Georgetown.

FRIENDSHIP FIRE

In the early days of the American experiment, fires were a daily danger, to be fought by landowners and any nearby neighbors. Delaware's first organized fire company was created in 1775, pre-statehood, and was the precursor to today's volunteer fire company system, which is influential in Delaware's small towns.

Friendship Fire in Wilmington was formed around a simple idea: The sixty-three original members would each purchase two leather buckets and one wicker basket. When an alarm was sounded, they would put a candle in their window and head to the blaze, there to form a bucket brigade to the closest source of water. The company's initial apparatus was made up of seventy-four buckets but quickly gained a hand-pump engine from a French ship. Organizing efforts faltered during the Revolutionary War, but by the 1780s members resolved to recruit actively and strengthen the company.

In 1801, a fire erupted along East Fourth Street while the men of Friendship Fire were occupied in New Castle at the election. Women took their place on the line of the brigade and pumped the engine. "They did their work so faithfully that a general conflagration was averted," historian John Scharf wrote. His *History of Delaware* lists fires breaking out at newspapers, dry-goods stores, foundries and paper mills. Also struck were a church, a hotel, a soap and candle factory, a wire works, a cotton mill and a woolen mill, just to list a small representative sample.

The Friendship Fire Company predated American independence, founded in 1775. The sixty-three original members would bring leather pails to form a bucket brigade. *Delaware Public Archives*

The first firehouse was located on Fifth Street, between Shipley and Orange Streets, but moved to Seventh and Shipley by 1812. The officers included a president, secretary and treasurer, as well as four engineers and two bucket collectors. In 1825, the firehouse shifted to a one-story building on Market Street, between Sixth and Seventh, and moved to Orange Street in 1847.

Friendship celebrated its one hundredth anniversary with a bash in 1875 at the Masonic Temple and the Clayton House. As of 1888, Friendship boasted a brand-new La France fire engine, worth $4,100. It also had 1,600 feet of firehose, a four-story iron-fronted engine house worth $16,000 and eighty-seven members.

Other fire companies joined Friendship: Reliance, Brandywine, Delaware, Phoenix, Water Witch, Fame Hose, Washington and Weccacoe. Friendship Fire and its brothers served Wilmington until the 1920s, when the professional Wilmington Fire Department went into service.

9

RELIGION AND SCHOOLS

The stories of Delaware's churches and religious institutions could fill a book and have. The ones that we have selected here are representative of both the modern challenge of declining religious affiliation and of the diverse faiths that make Delaware a vibrant place to live. We also chose three schools with fascinating backstories—a crumbling 1700s schoolhouse, racist arsonists and an insistence on continuing segregation. (It's not what you think.)

LITTLE CREEK FRIENDS MEETING

The history of the religious life of the Society of Friends in Delaware is a fascinating one. The Friends thrived in decades past, but modern times have seen their numbers dwindle. One such illustrative example is that of the Little Creek Meeting, which operated from 1710 to 1888, though not always consistently.

The Little Creek meeting was an offshoot of the Duck Creek meeting, near Duck Creek north of Smyrna, which traced its roots to 1686. A Little Creek meetinghouse was built in 1771; prior to that, the Friends met in private homes. A new iteration of the meetinghouse, across the road from the older one, came around in 1802. The meeting was located about a mile northeast of Little Creek. The congregation held regular meetings until 1830, when it began alternating with Camden. In 1852, the two Creeks

An early Friends meeting outside of Dover, the Little Creek Meeting ran from 1710 to 1888. It was also home to a school for Black children. *Delaware Public Archives.*

reconnected—Duck Creek joined with Little Creek, a situation that lasted until approximately 1865. Thereafter, services were held only occasionally; the meetinghouse was sold in 1888.

A Quaker-run school for Black children was founded in 1881 and lasted until about 1893, with classes likely held in the meeting building.

A one-acre graveyard at the site, resting place for multiple generations of Friends, holds several hundred remains. The last person was buried there in 1945. In 2015, funds were raised and state support was pledged to build a new wall surrounding the burial grounds—a 631-foot block encirclement that replaced a crumbling brick outpost. The old marble caps from the prior wall were reused in the new one. The effort was led by the Camden Friends Meeting, which at the time had sixty members.

CHURCH OF JESUS CHRIST OF LATTER-DAY SAINTS

Latter-day Saints missionaries first entered the First State in 1837, but a congregation was not established in Delaware until 1918, in Wilmington.

For the first few years, the fledgling church held services at members' homes. In 1923, they began renting space, on Delaware Avenue, on West Street and then in the Odd Fellows building at Tenth and King Streets. Its final home was at 906 West Street, at the Pythian Castle Lodge, from 1932 to 1937. The first elder was Reed Smith, from 1918 to 1921.

The congregation heard from visitors and speakers over the years on various aspects of the faith. The president of the Eastern States Mission, George W. McCune, paid a visit in 1920. Following years brought a public lecture with photos from a stereopticon projector showing views of Salt Lake City, the Mormon Temple and the new Zion National Park; a discussion of "Is Mormonism Christian?" by Ada Fugal; and a lecture by an elder from Norristown, Pennsylvania, on "Experimenting with Life."

The final elder of the Wilmington congregation was Leo C. Christensen, from 1936 to 1937. He was promoted to East Penn District president and transferred to Pleasantville, New Jersey, in the second year. That would prove to be the end of the Saints church in Wilmington for several years.

CHRIST UMC

Religious institutions come and go—and go, as the exhaustive research of historian Frank Zebley and the Works Progress Administration make clear. Declining populations, religious preferences and leadership tussles all contributed to the decline of churches, synagogues and other houses of worship.

A representative story of the history of Methodism in Delaware is that of Christ United Methodist Church in Laurel—albeit a sad one. The story begins in the fall of 1831, when the Reverend Thomas Pearson arrived in the western Sussex County community. The burgeoning congregation held its early meetings in a schoolhouse and put up a church on West Street in 1832. The benches, lacking backs, were somewhat uncomfortable, and were upgraded to backed seats in 1841. A cemetery was located nearby; Zebley observes in his book on Delaware churches that the old graveyard could still be seen in the late 1940s and that the oldest gravestone was of Susan Townsend, who died in 1852.

Thirty years later, in 1866, the church purchased property on Wheat Street, now Central Avenue, the main thoroughfare running through town.

Though the church was founded in 1831, the stone façade of Christ United Methodist Church was a landmark on Laurel's Central Avenue starting in 1911. *Delaware Public Archives.*

The Laurel Methodist Protestant Church was built for $8,000. A two-story frame building went up there as the second church, and the West Street site was sold to a Black church. In 1911, construction began on an imposing stone edifice that would stand for more than one hundred years. The church was completed under the Reverend James H. Straughn in 1912. Straughn served until 1919 and was a leader in the Methodist unification movement.

The new Christ United Methodist expanded over the years, including in 2002, with a new educational wing, ADA accessibility features and bathrooms. In 2009, it launched an outreach ministry with free soup as a joint venture between the Reverend David Elzey and the Reverend Dale Dunning, head of the Jusst Sooup Ministry.

The church was feeling its age, however. Church leaders were planning to pay a mason to study the building construction, as the building plans from 1911–12 had gone missing sometime over the last century. Then on February 16, 2016, a chunk of stone veneer from the north tower wall fell into the parking lot below around 9:30 a.m. The mason and engineer were on site within a few hours. "We have been very conservative and so is our engineer to protect property and people," said Derby Walker, chair of the church trustees, in the church newsletter.

Crews began stabilizing the outer wall, and the engineer recommended that the congregation not use the organ or ring the bell. But the immediate work and church-bell cautions were not enough. About a year later, the building was being salvaged by a crew filming it for a DIY Network show, hauling pews, a bell and a skylight away. It was demolished sometime later. The end of Christ United Methodist was at hand.

CHESED SHEL EMETH

Delaware's Jewish population is small, with only an estimated 9,300 Jews statewide. But its history is rich and dynamic, with sagas of triumph and tragedy side by side. Today, there are synagogues in each county, with multiple houses of worship in the most populous, New Castle County. In the early years of the Jewish community, one such synagogue was Chesed Shel Emeth, located on Wilmington's Shipley Street. The Sephardic, yet unaffiliated, congregation was founded in 1901 by a minyan of thirteen men. Services were conducted in the home of Morris Chalkin on West Fourth Street for the first few years; from 1903 to 1915, they were held in the home of Rabbi Rillel Sabrisky on Shipley Street. High Holiday services and special occasions were marked at the local Polish community hall or the Odd Fellows' Hall.

Chesed Shel Emeth was a Sephardic but unaffiliated Jewish synagogue in Wilmington. Founded in 1901, it eventually declined and merged with Adas Kodesch. *Delaware Public Archives.*

In 1915, the congregation opened a stand-alone synagogue at 227 Shipley Street, a two-story brick building described as being in the "Moorish style." The cornerstone-laying ceremony featured multiple rabbis and the mayor of Wilmington, Harrison W. Howell. At the dedication ceremony, the congregation gathered at Sixth and French Streets and removed the Torah from the Ark to march to the new synagogue. A school annex went up in 1926. Chesed Shel Emeth also oversaw a Jewish chapel on Tatnall Street for funeral services for Jews who died with no relatives.

The community thrived for several decades, with vibrant social and religious activities. But apparently two Orthodox congregations were too much for a city of Wilmington's size. In 1957, Chesed Shel Emeth merged with Adas Kodesch, which was sixteen years older, founded in 1885. The combined synagogue worshiped at Adas Kodesch until a new building was constructed. About six hundred people participated in a march from Chesed Shel Emeth, "chanting ancient hymns and carrying the Scrolls of the Ark," a newspaper reported. Today, Adas Kodesch Shel Emeth is Delaware's traditional synagogue, standing active and vibrant at Washington Boulevard and Torah Way.

FORWOOD SCHOOL

The Forwood School opened for students more than two hundred years ago, carved out of the woods and painstakingly constructed with Delaware rock and lumber. The one-room schoolhouse was funded from receipts from state marriage and tavern licenses and named after two of its three founders, Robert and Jehu Forwood. Thomas Bird was the third. The teacher's salary was paid by local residents.

Students studied and learned at Forwood, located near Carrcroft, for generations. It was enlarged from a single room in 1845, and ten years later it was home to more than one hundred students.

In the 1920s, voters approved the building of a new school, but the Great Depression came along and cratered those plans until the state could approve the funds. Forwood was used as a school until 1939, when it was merged into the A.I. du Pont School District. It was the oldest public school in the state. A year later, the building was purchased by the Society for the Preservation of Antiquities, which tried but failed to raise money for its preservation as the nation turned to a war footing.

The Forwood School last held students in 1939, but plans are underway to create a replica building using its 1799 datestone. *Delaware Public Archives.*

It was sold back to the Forwood family in 1947, which used it as a house for several decades before it became vacant and run down. "It's custom, not mortar" supporting the building, local historian and descendant James Hanby said in 2018. It was in such poor condition that the roof completely caved in, and nothing from the interior could be saved.

The property was purchased by a developer in 2014, with eventual plans to construct a shopping center and thirty-eight-townhouse subdivision called Forwood Commons. The school site was demolished in the summer of 2023, with plans for a replica school building featuring the 1799 datestone and using other salvaged stones. At 224 years old, Forwood was the "oldest school still standing in the continental United States," according to a local journalist, Larry Nagengast, who chronicled the site for several years.

SLAUGHTER NECK SCHOOL

In 1867, the Black community of Slaughter Neck, near Milford, organized itself to construct a new public school. Classes had been held in the Methodist

Students play outside the rebuilt Slaughter Neck School in 1926. The original school burned in an arson in 1867. *Delaware Public Archives.*

Episcopal Church nearby; the new school building went up on land that had been rented for five dollars annually.

But just after the school had been finished, "the plastering hardly dry," a rampaging mob of white men swooped down on Slaughter Neck and torched the building. Investigators from the Freedmen's Bureau found "evidence very strong" against a group of young white men who were at a store the night of the fire speaking out against Black people who dared to educate themselves.

"No use to build a n—— school house. It shall not stand it shall be burned down," the suspected arsonists and absolute bigots boasted, according to the investigation report. The evidence, however strong, was not sufficient for a court of law. The arsonists went unpunished—but the school was rebuilt. "The scholars had not been frightened away but were in full force," an investigator, Major General E.M. Gregory, noted. "Over forty in their old church one [of] the most interesting schools I have visited."

Even after the Civil War, it was clear that southern Delaware had much progress to make to achieve equality under the law and in the classroom.

ROSS POINT SCHOOL

Due to widespread structural racism and official indifference, education for Black children in Delaware—particularly in Sussex County—lagged behind that of white children for many decades. In the late 1860s, Sussex County had 143 schools for white children but just two for Black children. By 1890, after Reconstruction had ended, there were just 28 schools for the Black population. Delaware's leaders of the time refused to ratify the Thirteenth, Fourteenth and Fifteenth Amendments, calling them "Negro Domination" and labeling their Democratic Party the "White Man's Party." The amendments were ratified in 1901 under Republican governor John Hunn, a Quaker, but very little changed in the way of education.

The Ross Point School narrative is a story of how leaders led and attitudes changed over the decades. It would take chemist and philanthropist Pierre S. du Pont to change things by organizing the Service Citizens of Delaware and putting $1.5 million into the group in 1918 ($32 million today). After the

The property for the Ross Point School, outside Laurel, was purchased for one dollar in 1922. In 1980, it was sold to the Ross Point Improvement Club, also for one dollar. *Delaware Public Archives.*

end of the Great War and the global flu epidemic, he led a project to invest in and rebuild all of Delaware's public schools, including schools for Black children to thrive and learn.

Ross Point was one of those schools, designated 215-C. The *C* stood for "Colored." While an early school founded outside Laurel is believed to have been founded around 1892, later known as the Old Ross Point School, the new Ross Point School property was purchased for $1 in 1922, including 3.4 acres of land. Du Pont's money went to build the new school for $6,300—about $115,000 today. The state board of education ran the school and provided teachers. There were twenty-five students that first year, many having to walk to school a mile or more.

Covered in cedar shingle siding and boasting a steel jungle gym, indoor toilets and a small kitchen, Ross Point was designed by James Betelle, who was the architect for many other Black schools in Delaware under the du Pont scheme. The building was angled so the sun did not hit students in the face, and windows permitted the teacher to open them from either the top or the bottom to boost ventilation. "His scrupulous attention to detail...reflects an attention to the comfort of students that was never before taken into account and was considered very progressive," historians noted in 2001.

Ross Point's teachers and students thrived for decades even as separate-but-equal laws made them second-class citizens. It never had fewer than twenty students. The final teacher at Ross Point was Cora Norwood Selby, from 1941 to 1964, when it was closed and folded into the Laurel School District. Perhaps surprising to readers of today, Norwood Selby and local residents fought the desegregation of Ross Point after the Supreme Court's 1954 ruling. Students received new textbooks and materials every year, and they understood more than most the white backlash that would take place after integration was accomplished.

From the 1960s on, Ross Point sat unused as surplus state property. In 1980, it was sold for one dollar to the Ross Point Improvement Club, which still owns it as of this writing. The building remained standing for many years but suffered from the ravages of time. A collapse of two floor joists caused the floor to settle a foot below the walls, and the rear door was boarded up; it burned down in 2007.

10
TRANSPORTATION

How we get around our state is a collective story of power, influence and technology. From railroads to bridges, airplanes to lighthouses, the places and artifacts that help us get from Point A to Point B have shaped Delaware for better and for worse. Some crumbled due to economic changes, others due to the strength of ice. All should have a place in our memory.

THE INLET BRIDGE

For several decades, the Indian River Inlet moved. A gap in a thin island between the Indian River Bay and the Atlantic Ocean, the inlet's position would shift and change with the storms—often opening after storms hit and then closing later after being filled with dirt and sand. It wasn't until 1939 that the U.S. Army Corps of Engineers finished its plan to stabilize and anchor the inlet in one place, building massive stone-and-steel jetties.

There have been five bridges over the inlet—four older ones and the current span—though not to match the five known locations of the inlet. The first was a wooden bridge built in 1934; it lasted only a handful of years due to deterioration from the salt in the water. The second was a swing bridge that opened in 1940, costing $165,900 (about $3.6 million today). It was wrecked by ravaging ice floes in 1948, carrying away a truck from the Electric Company of Philadelphia in its collapse; three workers were killed, including two who tried to rescue the driver. The third bridge, a swing span with two lanes, was built around 1952 but was heavily damaged during the devastating Storm of 1962 that violently assaulted the Delaware coast with all of nature's force.

Delaware's coast went without a bridge for three more years, when a steel girder bridge opened, the longest-lasting of the spans. A second parallel bridge opened to handle more vehicles in 1976, creating one bridge for northbound traffic and one for southbound. These bridges stood until 2012, when the most recent bridge was opened. It was designed as a cable-stay bridge with no footings in the water to reduce scouring and damage. There was much legal drama surrounding the development of the new bridge, as approach ramps made of earth began settling and the state had to scrap the original design. The current bridge opened to traffic in 2012, with blue lights serving as a bat-friendly beacon.

Four of the five bridges over the inlet have been named for Charles W. Cullen, an attorney and former chair of the State Highway Commission in the late 1930s. Most people, however, simply call it the Indian River Inlet Bridge.

This iteration of the Indian River Inlet Bridge, seen in 1975, was the fourth of its name. It was replaced with a more modern span in 2012. *Delaware Public Archives.*

VANISHED RAILROADS

The railroad in its multiple formats spurred the development of much of the First State. Railcars carried freight from farms to markets; some canning operations built railyards or sidings next to the tracks for efficiency. Passenger cars shepherded residents on vacations or to visit friends and family. They created connections between small towns and big cities in the days of the horse and buggy—not an inconsiderable accomplishment.

The railroad led to the creation of many towns and communities along the line. It led to the formation of the town of Viola, previously called Canterbury Station. The Breakwater and Frankford line connected the rural areas around the tiny community of Stockley, south of Georgetown, with big cities where farmers shipped their produce, including strawberries. Tiny Ellendale, in northern Sussex County, once boasted canneries, a sawmill, basket mills and a button factory thanks to the Junction and Breakwater railroad line. The J&B at one time went down the middle of Rehoboth Avenue in Rehoboth Beach, stopping short of the beach proper, ferrying passengers from Philadelphia and other points south to a coastal getaway in the cool salt air. Its name persists in a bike trail that runs between Lewes and Rehoboth.

Some railroad communities, such as Farmington, were once busy but declined as other towns, such as Harrington, surpassed them. The rail town of Lincoln City was designed as the Sussex County seat, but the plans never came to fruition, Lincoln City was never incorporated as a city and rail service halted there in the 1940s. Newark once boasted three separate railroads with three separate stations. And Milton, in northeastern Sussex, expanded from relying on the Broadkill River for commerce to a rail freight hub shipping grain, lumber and holly trees during Christmastime.

One rail tale comes to us handed down from the early era of Prohibition. A community in western Kent County, known as Hickman, had a tiny railroad station that served as a central point for canneries and farms surrounding the area. The station was also the lone tavern and restaurant. When the Delaware area went "dry," the story goes, local residents asked the railroad to move the station three hundred feet across the Maryland border to resume alcohol sales. It was indeed picked up and moved—but by residents, not the railroad.

As auto and air travel replaced railroads throughout the 1900s, there were attempts at revivals. One such try was the Blue Diamond line, which attempted an ill-fated launch in 1965. It ferried passengers from Delmar to

The village of Canterbury Station was founded due to its location along the railroad. It was later named Viola, now with a population of less than two hundred. *Delaware Public Archives.*

Wilmington and vice-versa, with two passenger cars. The first day, July 1, carried just sixteen passengers, and it never caught on after that. The Blue Diamond was shut down by the end of the year.

Today, the rail lines still ship freight, but the only passenger service is located in northern Delaware, taking people to Philadelphia and points north. The Wilmington & Western Railroad is a twenty-mile tourist run along some beautiful scenery. The stations in many small towns have been abandoned or torn down, seen only in photographs.

QUEEN ANNE PIER

The Queen Anne Railroad chugged along to its endpoint in Lewes for several decades in the late 1800s and early 1900s, running from Love Point in Kent Island, Maryland, on the Eastern Shore. Some railcars were built in Wilmington at the Jackson & Sharp manufacturing center.

The Queen Anne Pier, a scenic spot, was the final stop in Lewes. It jutted out 1,202 feet into the bay from Lewes Beach so the *Queen Caroline* ferry vessel could run between Lewes and Cape May, New Jersey, meeting the railroad passengers over the water. A pier superintendent collected five cents from visitors but was stymied by children who swam out to the end, climbed up and walked back—collecting nothing because they carried nothing in their bathing suits. The railroad closed in 1924, but the pier stayed, serving as an access point for fishermen and a refueling and water station for larger ships heading into the Atlantic.

In February 1936, large ice floes smashed into the pier, destroying the middle section. As the ice melted, one thousand feet of the pier broke off and began floating away. The pier custodian, Captain David Edwards, and his two sons-in-law attempted to lasso the floating portion to see what could be salvaged. A seven-thousand-gallon water tank was left standing at the far end.

The pier was rebuilt over the summer, but a final September storm proved its end. Two sections of the pier, totaling seventy feet long, were washed away. The Lewes boardwalk and several boats were also wrecked and several homes flooded. It was not rebuilt after that.

SMITH'S BRIDGE AND WOODDALE BRIDGE

Covered bridges evoke the quintessential country image of horses clip-clopping over creeks and streams underneath a temporary shelter, surrounded by woods and snow. Delaware has three remaining covered bridges, all in New Castle County—but only one is original.

The original Smith's Bridge, which is a stone's throw from the Pennsylvania state line, dates to 1839 and crosses the Brandywine Creek. It experienced truck damage and was prepared for being torn down in 1954, but earned a reprieve thanks to the appeal of state engineer William A. McWilliams. It was rebuilt with a steel deck and its wooden structure bolstered by stone piers in the water. But in 1961, around Halloween, the bridge was lost to arson, with Mischief Night vandals suspected. "Nearby residents said the fire seemed to start all at once," a newspaper reported. "Many firemen narrowly escaped injury as they picked their way around burned-out holes and cracks and ducked falling beams." An initial estimate at repairing the span put the cost at $75,000—more than $769,000 at the time of this writing. It took more than forty years and the efforts of a local civic association to rebuild. The 2002 bridge used Bongossi wood, a fire-resistant material from Africa.

Wooddale Bridge was built in 1850, crossing the Red Clay Creek. The village of Wooddale thrived for a time but emptied out after its last source of industry, a paper mill, burned in 1918. Wooddale Bridge lasted a bit longer, until 2003, when Tropical Storm Henri's flooding smashed it to pieces. The bridge's closure temporarily cut off 15 families from their homes. State authorities rebuilt the bridge from 2007 to 2008, raising the road above the

Red Clay by five feet and also using Bongossi wood for the bridge material. It reopened in December 2008.

Ashland Bridge, the lone original wooden structure, is one of thirteen bridges that once spanned the Red Clay. It's the smallest of the remaining trio, and—as a result of their destruction and rebuilding—the oldest, constructed in 1860. It's also known as Barley Mill Road Covered Bridge. It has been damaged multiple times—by trucks and from Hurricane Ida debris—but has always reopened. Ashland Bridge is near the Ashland Nature Center, operated by the Delaware Nature Society.

THE DELAPLANE

Robie Seidelinger was not a trained aircraft engineer. A typewriter company manager by trade, his hobby was building model planes—and he parlayed an intense fascination in aeronautics into his own aircraft in the early days of aviation.

Seidelinger moved from Maine to Wilmington in 1908 and was building away when, as the story goes, a friend put one of his models on display in a Market Street shop window in downtown Wilmington. The model sparked the attention of a men's clothing store owner, who joined together local worthies and business leaders to form the Wilmington Aero Club, or WAC, which began in February 1910. The goal was to get publicity and attention to Wilmington and eventually work around to holding air shows in the area.

At what is now Wawaset Park but was then called the Gentlemen's Driving Park, the group chose to start their efforts with Seidelinger building a biplane. It would be called the Delaplane, a fantastic name for the First State's first aircraft, and cost an estimated $6,000.

The Delaplane was built from spruce wood with cotton-covered wings and surfaces. The inventor weighed each plank, carved it and weighed it a second time; second pieces must mirror the weight precisely.

By August 1910, the body of the plane was finished. During taxi tests, Seidelinger discovered that changes needed to be made to his initial designs, including swapping out a single propeller for the original twins.

Local newspapers covered the ins and outs of the Delaplane development with intense interest. It got national attention in an aviation magazine, *Fly*. For an aviation-hungry society and media, the prospect was enticing.

Early plans were to have the plane in the air at an October air show in Wilmington: "Should the young bird show remarkable aptitude and the motor be consistent, these experienced aviators may permit it to hop," a Wilmington newspaper wrote. Several days of foul weather forced the cancellation of the multi-day event before the fledgling aircraft could make a flight attempt.

On October 21, during another round of taxiing tests, test pilot Eddie Bloomfield steered the Delaplane into the sky, picking up a few feet from the ground and flying for many yards. Delaware's first airplane had flown! As the *Wilmington Morning News* described it the next day:

> *Just as the shades of night were gathering Bloomfield tilted the front or lifting plane a few inches and the machine shot upward until a height of five feet was reached. Then leveling the plane, the aviator continued for forty or fifty yards before alighting…It was Bloomfield's first trip in an airship, and he could not express his feeling when spoken to about it afterwards, but he, like all those present, was very much pleased.*

The Delaplane flew several more times under Bloomfield's piloting. In 1911, on one occasion, he steered it fifty feet high and stayed aloft for twenty

Inventor Robie Seidelinger created Delaware's first homegrown aircraft, the Delaplane. It burned when lightning struck its barn in 1911. *Courtesy of the Delaware Historical Society.*

minutes. "Bloomfield seemed a little nervous in his descents," one newspaper noted—as well one might in a homemade flying machine crafted of wood and cloth.

The plane was later moved to a site at Hare's Corner deemed more suitable for follow-up flights, towed to the new location by horses. One flight there, in front of a few hundred people in July, flopped completely, as the plane fell from a height of about twenty feet and damaged some rods.

Alas, the Delawareans' dreams for the Delaplane did not survive. While the plane was under cover of a New Castle shed in 1911, the building was hit by a bolt of lightning and burned, as did the wood-and-cotton contraption inside. Seidelinger's plans did not survive to the modern day.

BELLANCA AIRFIELD

From Italy to America, Giuseppe Bellanca would leave his mark on the world as a brilliant engineer and inventor. His legacy in Delaware? Three thousand airplanes built on First State soil, turning tiny New Castle into a center of aviation innovation.

Bellanca found his way to Delaware after work as a flying instructor, designing biplanes and creating a groundbreaking four-passenger monoplane, the renowned Bellanca CF. Charles Lindbergh wanted to fly a CF on his nonstop Atlantic flight, but Bellanca's financial supporters refused to sell it. A CF ultimately set the trans-Atlantic distance record a few weeks after Lindbergh, traveling 301 more miles than the *Spirit of St. Louis*.

After a prior business partnership failed, Bellanca and Henry B. du Pont formed a deal that would lead to a new airfield and aircraft factory at the 360-acre Spring Garden Farm in New Castle. Within a year, the new Bellanca Airfield would include two hangars, offices and shops for engineering and assembly, woodworking and paint and fabric work. Two grass runways were laid out with the help of 3,500 pounds of grass seed and three tons of fertilizer. It opened to pomp and circumstance on October 6, 1928, with a twenty-nine-aircraft flight winging over the airfield.

The venture relied most importantly on Giuseppe Bellanca's intellect and vision, which were considerable. "I was thoroughly convinced that Bellanca not only was a genius but a hero of a rare sort," pilot Clarence Chamberlin wrote in 1928, seven years after flying one of his early aircraft.

Giuseppe Bellanca (*center with bowtie*) presents a Bellanca aircraft to the Delaware State Police in 1932. Business partner Henry B. du Pont is second from right. *Delaware Public Archives.*

Bellanca sold planes to the U.S. Navy, air show pilots, the government of Colombia, small regional airlines and the Chinese side in the Second Sino-Japanese War. It attempted to sell to the Republican/leftist side in the Spanish Civil War, but that attempt was blocked by the U.S. government. The Delaware plant turned out new "short takeoff and landing" planes and training aircraft for the U.S. Army Air Corps during World War II. It also built aircraft parts for other manufacturers—gas tanks, flaps, wing floats, ailerons and engine cowlings, among others. The plant employed three thousand workers at its peak.

After the war, despite initial giddy predictions about a boom for privately owned aircraft, demand faltered and the market had a glut of airplanes. Bellanca turned to its new Crusair plane, but Beechcraft produced a superior similar but cheaper model, the Bonanza. The Bellanca plant was unionized by the United Auto Workers, sales slipped and the company's finances fell. By 1950, production was so far down that Bellanca laid off many workers. The final plane that came off the New Castle production lines was the Cruisemaster, of which 103 were sold.

Workers at the Bellanca aircraft manufacturing plant do some of the fine work on smaller parts the planes required. *Delaware Public Archives*

Giuseppe Bellanca sold the company in 1954; he sold the plant and land to Pennsylvania-based Piasecki Helicopters of Pennsylvania in 1956. He moved from Delaware to an 1860s estate known as Shorewood on the Eastern Shore of Maryland, but his dream and vision of better aircraft did not falter. He continued work at home with his son, August, under the name AviaBellanca Inc., on a new plane called the Skyrocket (also known as the Skyrocket II), an all-fiberglass composite.

In 1960, the four-hundred-acre airfield was sold to a developer with plans to build housing and commercial space on the site. There were about fifteen private planes based at the airport by then, most of which were moved to Summitt Aviation near Middletown, at Baker Field. A few years later, the town of New Castle would have a significant problem with illicit drag racing at the shuttered property, charging more than seventy-five people in a single weekend.

Less than a month later, Bellanca himself died after being diagnosed with leukemia. He was seventy-four. He never saw his Skyrocket II completed, though son August did; it set multiple world speed records. Guiseppe Bellanca was inducted into the National Aviation Hall of Fame posthumously in 1993. August Bellanca died in 2010.

Today, the hangar at the Bellanca Airfield site is being restored by a Friends organization, houses the Delaware Aviation Hall of Fame and is open to the public; visit http://www.bellancamuseum.org for details.

PORT MAHON LIGHT

Jane Elizabeth Little and her eight siblings lived the dream: they grew up in a lighthouse.

Her father was a real, honest-to-goodness lighthouse keeper, and her mother organized the children and polished the brass fixtures. The kids? They walked three miles across the marsh to school each day from their remote outpost on the Delaware Bay.

The only full-time residents of Port Mahon, Lynch family members staffed the lighthouse for nearly thirty years, starting in 1912. The Lynches previously served in lighthouses at 14 Foot Bank, near Lewes, and Reedy Point, near Augustine Beach.

The Port Mahon light in which Jane Little grew up was just one in a series of lighthouses serving the oystermen of Kent County and shipping in the Delaware Bay channels. Four previous houses, dating to 1831, were described as "badly built" or "threatened with early destruction" due to erosion. One station, valued at $4,000 in 1903 dollars, was purchased at auction by a Little Creek neighbor for $350.

The lighthouse with the longest time in service was first lit in June 1903 and would be the last manned station there. It was a connection between the oystermen of Port Mahon and the land, with wife Janie Lynch often providing sustenance—"beans and biscuits"—to the oystermen during harsh winters when their boats were frozen to the docks. "And any tramp that came along, she never turned him down. She fed him, too," Jane Little recalled.

On land, the family had a barn with horses and, later, a 1914 Ford, to transport their cargo along the oyster shell road to Little Creek. The pay was forty-nine dollars a month, though the federal government sent quantities of essentials like wood, oil, coal and hardtack crackers.

Like too many artifacts of Delaware history, the Port Mahon lighthouse burned after sitting empty. "We loved it there," recalled Jane Little, whose family lived there for years. *Delaware Public Archives.*

Little married and moved away—though not far, just to Little Creek—in 1920. Her father, Irvin S. Lynch Sr., passed away shortly after retiring in 1939, and her mother died at age 77 in 1954. The light was automated after Irvin Lynch's death, and the lighthouse was closed in 1955. A replacement tower went up close by.

The U.S. Coast Guard offloaded the Port Mahon Light property to the U.S. Air Force for a pipeline facility to take jet fuel from barges to Dover Air Force Base. By the 1980s, the land had been declared surplus and sold to a private pipeline company.

Plans were discussed to restore the lighthouse by preservationists and local residents, but they never came to fruition. It was added to the National Register of Historic Places in 1976, but that didn't protect it from enterprising vandals who stole the cast-iron stove, the brass globe on the cupola and the sliding doors.

One night in 1984, the long-abandoned lighthouse caught ablaze. Firefighters raced to the scene, alerted by a watchman at a nearby storage depot, but were too late; it fell into the bay shortly after they arrived. "It was totally orange, and flames were shooting out the windows," said deputy Leipsic fire chief Horace E. Pugh. "There is nothing there but pilings now, and some of them are still smoldering."

A few weeks after the fire, Jane Elizabeth Little chatted with a newspaper reporter about her memories of life at the light. Some family members had shed tears hearing of the burning of their former home. "When my sister Ethel heard it, she just cried and cried," Jane Little said. "'There's so many things we remember there,' she said. And I said, 'Stop crying. It's just an old house, and it's gone now.' But we loved it there."

CAPE HENLOPEN LIGHT

For more than 160 years, a lighthouse stood as sentinel at Cape Henlopen, the point that marks the confluence of the Atlantic Ocean and the Delaware Bay. It was a permanent addition to the coastal skyline for generations of residents—until it wasn't.

"It had really become a member of the family in many homes," Lewes historian Hazel Brittingham told the *Cape Gazette* newspaper in 2016, on the ninetieth anniversary of the lighthouse's fall. "It seems strange to say that, but it was almost personified."

The lighthouse was constructed at the request of Philadelphians who wanted to guard ships and cargo from being beached as they sailed into the Delaware Bay. Delaware was still part of Pennsylvania at the time, and Richard and Thomas Penn allowed the legislature to take two hundred acres of coastal land for the lighthouse in 1762. It was completed five years later, erected atop the Great Dune. At 87 feet tall, it towered over the Atlantic by 130 feet and featured a thick rock exterior and wood interior. The light itself was lit by whale oil, later changing to mineral oil or lard.

The lighthouse had been precariously balanced over the edge of the Great Dune for some time, with observers noting the impact of building a structure on shifting sand as early as 1788: "Every precaution should therefore be taken to secure the foundation from the growing effect of this evil," the board responsible for its upkeep reported.

In 1905, brush was placed at the base to protect it from erosion, an attempt similar to modern-day sand or snow fences. Local flooding from

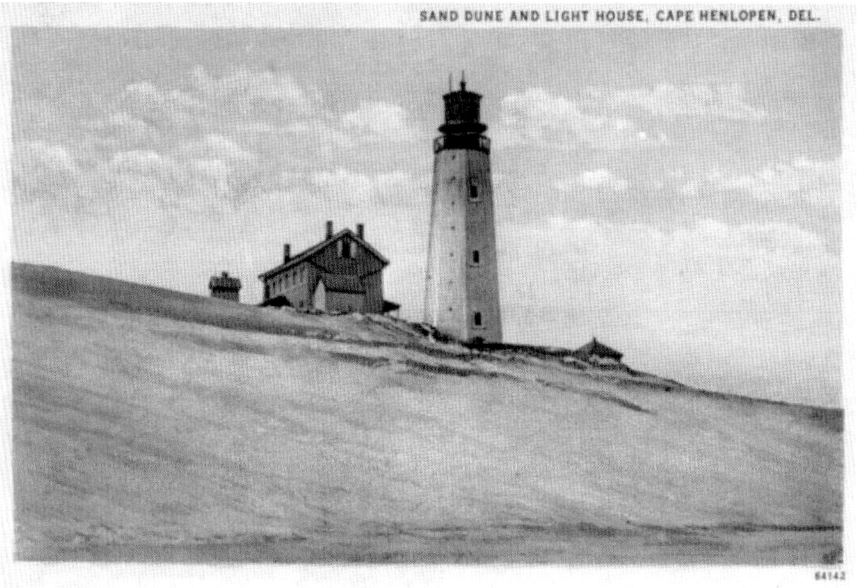

The Cape Henlopen Lighthouse was the victim of its own foundation, as the shifting sands of the Atlantic beach created its downfall. *Delaware Public Archives.*

a January 1914 storm cut off the lighthouse from the rest of the town. By 1924, the government built its Plan B—a "temporary skeleton steel tower" nearby that would be lit if the lighthouse were to fall. On October 1, the light was extinguished permanently.

In the spring of 1926, Coast Guard patrols preemptively blocked off access to the area for safety in anticipation of its collapse. The lighthouse toppled over in an instant on April 13. Around 12:45 p.m., the final grain of sand shifted—perhaps due to strong winds that day—and the structure slid and fell down to the beach. Part of the lighthouse tower "was smashed almost to powder," and the former housing for the light "was a twisted mass of metal," one newspaper reported.

The local telephone switchboard was flooded, with local residents calling out and journalists and artists calling in. "The entire force of young women operators in Lewes were required for several hours to handle the telephone connections caused by the emergency," a Wilmington newspaper said.

After the lighthouse's collapse, Lewes residents swarmed the rubble on the beach and carried away stone and other materials. "One man is reported to have half filled his automobile with stones from the structure and driven off," one paper reported. Today, the scavenged lighthouse stone makes up parts of many area buildings, such as the fireplaces in Lewes City Hall.

BIBLIOGRAPHY

Greenabaum Cannery

Cape Gazette. "Tomato Season Then and Now in Sussex County." July 21, 2020. https://www.capegazette.com.

Delaware Gazette and State Journal. "Seaford." September 14, 1899.

Journal Every-Evening. "Cannery Head of Seaford Dies." May 25, 1940.

———. "Cannery Worker Burned." August 1, 1938.

———. "Sussex Music Master Dies; Turned from Canning to Art." March 22, 1938.

———. "$25,000 Fire Sweeps Warehouse of Greenabaum Bros., Seaford." May 10, 1948.

Kee, Ed. *Saving Our Harvest: The Story of the Mid-Atlantic Region's Canning and Freezing Industry*. Baltimore: CTI Publications Inc., 2006.

Middletown Transcript. "From Old Sussex." January 11, 1896.

———. "From Old Sussex." October 19, 1895.

———. "Old Sussex." June 25, 1898.

Morning News. "Canning Factory Improvements." November 1, 1898.

———. "News of the Peninsula." June 14, 1897.

———. "Seaford Canner Called by Death." January 18, 1924.

———. "Three Funerals Held in Seaford." January 22, 1924.

———. "Wheatley Family Reunion Thursday." August 16, 1938.

Smyrna Times. June 10, 1896.

Strawberry Fields

Kee, Ed. *Delaware Farming.* Charleston, SC: Arcadia Publishing, 2007.
Morgan, Michael. "A New Highway Fueled Strawberry Revival in Sussex County." *Daily Times (Salisbury, MD)*, May 10, 2019. https://www.delmarvanow.com.
U.S. Census of Agriculture. "Berries by Acres: 2017." April 11, 2019. https://www.nass.usda.gov.

The Cows of Winterthur

Holland, Hillary. "Breeding the Best: The Dairy Herd at Winterthur." Winterthur Museum, Garden & Library. July 31, 2023. winterthur.org.
Material Matters. "Going with the Goats." November 12, 2018. https://sites.udel.edu.
Maynard, W. Barksdale. "Winterthur Farms Dairy Buildings." SAH Archipedia. https://sah-archipedia.org.

King Street Market

Cooper, Constance J. *To Market, To Market, in Wilmington: King Street and Beyond.* Wilmington, DE: Cedar Tree Press, 1993.
Downtown Visions. "Downtown Farmer's Market." May 3, 2023. http://downtownwilmingtonde.com.

Chipman Sweet Potato House

Biden School of Public Policy & Administration Center for Historic Architecture and Design. "Remembering Buildings of the Past." https://www.bidenschool.udel.edu.
Hoey, Kim. "Sussex Gave Rise to Sweet Potato House." *News Journal*, April 3, 1991.
National Register of Historic Places. "Chipman Sweet Potato House." https://npgallery.nps.gov.
Tyson, Rae. "Potato Houses Offer Glimpse into Rich Farm History." Delmarva Now. January 21, 2016. https://www.delmarvanow.com.

Wilmington Dry Goods

Frank, Bill. "Letter to Lazarus." *Morning News*, December 7, 1978.

Frank, William P. "Services for Marketing Genius J.M. Lazarus Held in California." *Morning News*, January 16, 1981.

Frank, William P., and Mary Rowland. "Wilmington Dry to Shut Doors of Downtown Store." *Morning News*, December 5, 1979.

Jewish Historical Society of Delaware. "Half a Chance: Stories of Jewish Delawareans." https://jhsdelaware.org.

Burton Brothers Hardware

Diehl, James. "Call the Marvels." *Morning Star Business Report*, October 2008. https://issuu.com.

Fisher, James. "Burton Bros. Store Closing Its Doors." *News Journal*, January 26, 2013.

———. "Historic Store Is Demolished." *Delaware Wave*, June 25, 2013.

———. "History, Up in Flames." *News Journal*, November 14, 2021.

National Park Service. "Burton Hardware Store." National Register of Historic Places Nomination Form. November 18, 1977. https://npgallery.nps.gov.

Soulsman, Gary. "Honor Thy Brothers: Seaford Residents Organize Tribute to Hardware Store." *News Journal*, March 11, 2021.

Ninth Street Book Shop

Alamdari, Natalia. "Meet the Woman Writing a New Chapter for Wilmington's book scene." *News Journal*, September 30, 2021. https://www.delawareonline.com.

Burkes, Catie. "What Will Happen to 9th Street Book Shop?" *News Journal*, August 6, 2017.

Neiburg, Jeff. "Ninth Street Book Shop Closes Doors." *News Journal*, January 31, 2018.

Themal, Harry. "Bookshop Closure Is End of an Era." *News Journal*, August 14, 2017.

Tri-State Mall

Evening Journal. "Naamans Mall Work to Start." November 4, 1967.

Holveck, Brandon. "After Five Decades in Claymont, Tri-State Mall to Be Demolished This Summer and Replaced with a Warehouse." *News Journal*, March 15, 2022, www.delawareonline.com.

Mammarella, Ken. "One Store's Still Standing at Tri-State Mall." Town Square Delaware. January 23, 2023. https://townsquaredelaware.com.

Morning News. "New Motion Picture Theater Plan Announced." December 17, 1968.

———. "Wilmington Dry to Build Store Mall." October 15, 1964.

Nazarewycz, Michael J. *Historic Movie Theaters of Delaware.* Charleston, SC: The History Press, 2019.

Blue Hen Mall

Brooks, Jane. "Bank Gives Reasons for Picking Kent." *News Journal*, April 27, 1995.

———. "Blue Hen Mall: There May Be Life in the Old Bird Yet." *News Journal*, September 3, 1994.

Nazarewycz, Michael J. *Historic Movie Theaters of Delaware.* Charleston, SC: The History Press, 2019.

Pettinaro. "Blue Hen Corporate Center." https://pettinaro.com.

Tahmincioglu, Eve. "Rose's Closes Dover Store as Sales End." *News Journal*, March 19, 1994.

National Bank of Wilmington and Brandywine

Delaware Gazette. "Wilmington & Brandywine Bank." March 24, 1810.

Delaware Genealogy Trails. "Washington Jones & Co." http://genealogytrails.com.

"Eastern States." *Bankers Magazine*, 1913.

Epstein, Jonathan, "Anchor for State Has Seen Its Share of Ups and Downs." *News Journal*, June 29, 2003.

Frank, William. "Farmers Bank Stood Firm at Same Site." *News Journal*, April 11, 1982.

Hoffecker, Carol E. *Brandywine Village: The Story of a Milling Community.* Wilmington, DE: Old Brandywine Village Inc., 1974.

Morning News. "George S. Capelle, Veteran Banker, Dies at 94 Years." September 24, 1929.

The Rigbie Hotel

Marvel McNaught, Shannon. "Fire Displaces 54 People from Laurel Apartment Building, Once a Historic Hotel." *News Journal*. January 28, 2022. https://www.delawareonline.com.

Russo, Tony. "Memories of a Lost Rigbie Hotel and the Old Laurel Downtown." *Andrew Sharp*. November 15. https://www.andrewsharp.net.

Happy Harry's

Church, Steven. "'I'm Shocked': Longtime Workers, Customers Caught Off Guard by Sale." *News Journal*, June 6, 2006.

Cormier, Ryan. "Happy Harry Is Back? Yes, but Not as the Beloved, Long-Gone Delaware Pharmacy Chain." *News Journal*, February 14, 2023. https://www.delawareonline.com.

Griffith, Ted. "Del. Chain Felt Need for Clout." *News Journal*, June 6, 2006.

Legacy. "Diane Levin Obituary." July 8, 2008. www.legacy.com.

Levin, Alan. "Harry Levin, Founder of Happy Harry's." *Delaware Today*. March 14, 2012. https://delawaretoday.com.

News Journal. "Happy Harry's through the Years." June 6, 2006.

WHYY. "Happy Harry's Is Another Delaware Name Ready to Sail Off into the Sunset." May 11, 2011. https://whyy.org.

The Wagon Wheel

Brooks, Jane. "To Many, Muskrat Is a Local Delicacy." *News Journal*, March 7, 1988.

Talorico, Patricia. "Diner's Digest: Ice Cream Fest on Food Network Monday." *News Journal*, September 10, 2014.

———. "How to Eat Fried 'Rat." *News Journal*, January 28, 2009.

———. "Turn for Help: The Wagon Wheel in Smyrna Called on Food Network's Robert Irvine for Restaurant Renovations." *News Journal*, May 18, 2013.

Kirby & Holloway

Brown, Jeff, "Owners Move Landmark Kirby & Holloway Restaurant Closer to Opening." *News Journal*, August 5, 2014. www.delawareonline.com.

Delaware Public Archives. "Delaware Snapshot: Recalling a Lost Landmark." Facebook, November 24, 2018. https://www.facebook.com.

Jackson, Patrick, "Dover Gets Role in Lieberman Ad." *News Journal*, October 26, 2003.

Mace, Ben. "Iconic Sign for Destroyed Dover Restaurant Lives On, Even Though the Site Has a New Owner." *News Journal*, September 13, 2021. https://www.delawareonline.com.

Min, Shirley. "Future of Delaware Diner in Question." WHYY. October 2, 2015. https://whyy.org.

Norton, Holly. "The Big Challenge: Getting There." *News Journal*, May 26, 2004.

Offredo, Jon. "Dover Boosts Eatery Staff." *News Journal*, February 15, 2014.

Rykiel, Walt. "Kent GOP Fund Taken Charged by Buckson." *News Journal*, March 31, 1972.

Sanginiti, Terri. "Fire Damage Exceeds $1M." *News Journal*, February 4, 2014.

Staff. "Kent County Icons: Kirby & Holloway Family Restaurant." *Delaware Today*, February 7, 2013. https://delawaretoday.com.

The Chuck Wagon

Ruth, Eric. "Old Chuck Wagon Site Faces Wrecking Ball." *News Journal*, March 17, 2007.

The Nanticoke Queen

Boston Globe. "Offer of Island to Government." March 6, 1917.

Brooklyn Daily Eagle. "McKeever Brothers Sued by Counsel." October 10, 1917.

Dekom, Otto. "Maybe They Just Hit an Off-Day." *Morning News*, February 10, 1980.

———. "Shipboard Eating beside U.S. 13." *Sunday News Journal*, March 20, 1977.

Dickerson, Howard. "Sunday Dinner at the Flagship." Delmar Historical and Art Society, November 24, 2019. https://delmarhistoricalandartsociety.blogspot.com.

Dictionary of American Naval Fighting Ships. "McKeever Bros (S. P. 683)." February 9, 2016. https://www.history.navy.mil.
Malone, Tom. "Licensed Trip." *Morning News*, November 17, 1969.
Miller, Ted. "The Nautical Décor Is a Natural." *Morning News*, September 27, 1969.
Morning News. "Fire Sweeps the Flagship Restaurant." April 12, 1977.
Murray, Molly. "Sussex Tentatively Oks Bonds for Two Businesses." *Morning News*, April 28, 1982.
Radigan, Joseph M. "McKeever Bros. (SP 683)." NavSource Online. http://www.navsource.org.
Ruth, Eric. "Nautico Reels in Landlubbers with Hearty Fare." *News Journal*, September 10, 1999.
Sussex County Government. Property Tax Records for 8805 Concord Road, Seaford, DE, Parcel 132-1.00-23.00, 8805. https://sussexcountyde.gov/property-tax-information.
Talorico, Patricia. "Dockside Dining." *News Journal*, October 1, 1999.
Trento, Joe. "Investigators Say $150,000 Fire at Flagship Restaurant Was Arson." *Evening Journal*, April 12, 1977.
Virginian-Pilot. "Sale of U. S. Naval Vessels." April 9, 1919.

The Diamond State Drive-In

Cinema Treasures. "Diamond State Drive-in." https://cinematreasures.org/theaters/9710.
Gibson, Ginger. "Drive-in Movie Era Ends in Delaware." *News Journal*, November 30, 2008.
Maltsev, Michael. "Felton, Delaware: Last Drive-In Theater Still Showing Outdoor Movies in Felton, Delaware."
New York Film Academy. "The History of Drive-in Movie Theaters." May 27, 2023. https://www.nyfa.edu.
Open Air Cinema. October 21, 2008. https://www.openaircinema.us.

Punkin Chunkin

Holveck, Brandon, "From a Bet among Friends to a Delaware Tradition." *News Journal*, May 29, 2019.
Horn, Brittany, "Punkin Chunkin Show Cut." *News Journal*, November 23, 2016.

Kenney, Ed. "P(umpkin) Shooters." *News Journal*, November 4, 1994.
Kipp, Rachel. "The Right Stuff." *News Journal*, November 5, 2007.
McNaught, Shannon Marvel. "Punkin Chunkin Has Eye on Maryland, Virginia." *News Journal*, November 10, 2021.
Price, Betsy. "Tidbits of Punkin Chunkin Lore Add Meat to Lofty Tales of Epic Efforts." *News Journal*, November 4, 2005.
Punkin Chunkin. www.punkinchunkin.com.
Staff. "World Championship Punkin Chunkin Heads to Oklahoma." News on 6. September 2, 2023. https://www.newson6.com.

Wheeler Park

Finney, Mike. "Kent County's Wheeler Park Comes Full Circle." *Delaware State News*, October 7, 2022. https://baytobaynews.com.
Morning News. "Obituaries: William A. Wheeler." May 21, 1984.

Brandywine Springs

The Friends of Brandywine Springs. http://www.fobsde.org/index.html.
German, Myna. "History Matters: A Sample of Brandywine Springs Amusement Park Sites." Delaware Public Media. October 28, 2016. www.delawarepublic.org.
Mill Creek Hundred History. "Brandywine Springs Amusement Park," September 7, 2010. http://mchhistory.blogspot.com,
Pauly, Megan. "History Matters: Brandywine Springs Park's Hidden Past as Natural Springs Resort." Delaware Public Media. September 30, 2016. https://www.delawarepublic.org.
———. "History Matters: Unearthing Brandywine Springs' Historic Amusement Park." Delaware Public Media. October 26, 2016. https://www.delawarepublic.org.

The Stone Balloon

Barrish, Cris. "Goodbye to a Bit of History." *News Journal*, December 18, 2005.
Besso, Michele. "Stone Balloon May Soon Serve Its Last Drink." *News Journal*, September 18, 2004.

Bowersox, Bob. "The Stone Balloon Floats Again Tonight." *Morning News*, July 19, 1985.

Brown, Donna. "Glory Days." *News Journal*, August 5, 1996.

Cormier, Ryan. "Balloon Animals." *News Journal*, November 12, 2004.

———. "The Balloon Ride Is Over." *News Journal*, December 16, 2005.

———. "The New 'Balloon' Is Aloft." *News Journal*, March 6, 2009.

———. "Stone Balloon Back on Main Street." *News Journal*, February 7, 2015.

———. "33 Favorite Delaware Concert Memories." *News Journal*, April 23, 2017.

Kenney, Ed. "Ex-Owner Preserves Stone Balloon Legacy." *News Journal*, August 23, 2005.

Markovetz, Jessie. "Behind the Stone Balloon." *University of Delaware Review*, November 21, 2006.

McCave, Marta. "Stone Balloon Officers Indicted on Federal Tax Charges." *Morning News*, April 14, 1982.

Newark Bureau Staff. "Stone Balloon to Expand." *News Journal*, June 20, 1972.

Panyard, Jim. "Stone Balloon: Will It Fly?" *News Journal*, September 27, 1971.

Stevenson, Bill. "The Stone Balloon Is Rich with Rock 'n' Roll Memories." *News Journal*, September 25, 2004.

Three Little Bakers

Focus Delaware. "Three Little Bakers Country Club Restaurant and Dinner Theater." August 4, 1983. Retrieved from YouTube. https://www.youtube.com/watch?v=-xmEhERiuTM.

Hess, Maria. "Can the Show Go On?" *Delaware Today*, June 8, 2009. https://delawaretoday.com.

Mullinax, Gary. "Shake & Bake." *News Journal*, January 19, 1996.

Myers, Brad, and Christopher Yasiejko. "Three Little Bakers to Close Theater Operations." *News Journal*, February 22, 2007.

News Journal. "Three Little Bakers to Open Largest Unit Here Tomorrow." February 15, 1956.

Talorico, Patricia. "The Last of the 'Three Little Bakers.'" DelawareOnline/*News Journal*, September 17, 2014. https://www.delawareonline.com.

Yasiejko, Christopher. "Three Little Bakes Unveils Christmas Show at Baby Grand." *News Journal*, August 10, 2007.

Kahunaville

Brown, Robin. "Club's Volcano Nearly Extinct." *News Journal*, September 18, 2009.

Cormier, Ryan. "Big Kahuna Returns for One Weekend." *News Journal*, April 5, 2013.

———. "Kahunaville Closed 12 Years Ago, but There's Still One More Party." DelawareOnline/*News Journal*, April 5, 2018. https://www.delawareonline.com.

———. "Kahunaville's Abrupt End Surprises Customers, City." *News Journal*, November 29, 2006.

Goldblatt, Jennifer. "Kahunaville Sells Five Restaurants." *News Journal*, July 3, 2004.

Hayden, Bill. "The Bigger Kahuna." *News Journal*, April 18, 1996.

Nolan, E. Janene. "Kahunaville Expands Overseas." *News Journal*, May 15, 2002.

Jason Beach

Contant, George, and Tim Miller. "Jason Beach at Trap Pond." Delaware State Parks. https://destateparks.com.

Delaware State Parks. "Jason Beach: A Gathering Place for Generations." https://destateparks.com.

Sharp, Andrew. "A New-Old Beach Name at Trap Pond Is Loaded with History." June 27, 2022. www.andrewsharp.net.

Rosedale Beach

Dixon, Mark E. "The Stories Behind 5 Famous Delaware Resorts of Yesteryear." *Delaware Today*, August 15, 2017. https://delawaretoday.com.

Haney, Abby. "Program Details Lost History of Rosedale Beach." *Delaware State News*, February 9, 2019. https://baytobaynews.com.

Parks, Lynn. "The Rosedale Refuge." *Delaware Beach Life*, August 2017.

The Clippers

Gelbert, Doug. *The Great Delaware Sports Book.* Montchanin, DE: Manatee Books, 1995.

Levin, Marty. "Clippers Score Easy 34 to 0 Win Over Fort DuPont." *Morning News*, November 10, 1941.

Morning News. "Clippers to Oppose Fort DuPont Eleven Here Tomorrow." November 8, 1941.

The Wilmington Quicksteps

Gelbert, Doug. *The Great Delaware Sports Book.* Montchanin, DE: Manatee Books, 1995.

Springer, Jon. *Once Upon a Team: The Epic Rise and Historic Fall of Baseball's Wilmington Quicksteps.* New York: Sports Publishing, 2018.

The Cypress Sawmill at Trap Pond

Journal-Every Evening. "U.S. Recreation Center, Lake Near Delmar, Grows Popular." June 21, 1941.

Koth, William. "History of Trap Pond State Park." Delaware State Parks Adventure Blog. April 22, 2020. https://destateparks.blog.

Murray, Molly. "Trap Pond No Longer Open to Swimmers." *News Journal*, May 18, 2000.

Bancroft Mill

Bancroft Mills Homeowners Association. "Bancroft Mills History." https://bancroftmills.com.

Bretzger, William, and Brittany Horn, Brittany. "Abandoned Bancroft Mills in Wilmington Burns." *News Journal*, November 10, 2016.

Neiburg, Jeff. "Part of Bancroft Mills Razed on Sunday." *News Journal*, October 16, 2017.

Staff. "Former Bancroft Mills Burns." *News Journal*, May 3, 2015.

Superfine Brandywine

Delaware Tribune. "Wilmington Markets." February 17, 1870.

Hoffecker, Carol. *Brandywine Village: The Story of a Milling Community.* Wilmington, DE: Old Brandywine Village Inc., 1974.

Lea Mills

Hagley Museum and Library. "Thomas Lea's Mills." www.hagley.org.

———. "William Lea & Sons, Co." www.hagley.org.

Hoffecker, Carol. *Brandywine Village: The Story of a Milling Community.* Wilmington, DE: Old Brandywine Village Inc., 1974.

Rockwell Center for American Visual Studies. "(1950) Lea Mills." https://www.frankschoonover.org.

duPont Motors

Evening Journal. "Du Pont Motors to Build New Plant." March 4, 1920.

———. "duPont Motors to Move." September 2, 1920.

———. "DuPonts to Begin First Auto Engine." August 18, 1919.

———. "New du Pont Auto Shown in New York." November 17, 1919.

———. "To Complete First Auto by November." August 18, 1919.

Girdler, Allan. *The Harley-Davidson and Indian Wars.* New York: Quarto, 2016.

Hickman, Emmett S. "For Sale or Rent: The Modern Plant." *Every Evening*, February 14, 1931 (advertisement).

Morning News. "New Firm Will Make 'duPont Automobile.'" July 7, 1919.

———. "Three duPont Models to Be Ready in July." May 8, 1920.

Wilson, W. Emerson. "Only 537 du Pont Cars Built." *Evening Journal*, June 17, 1968.

Newark Chrysler Plant

Bunkley, Nick. "Fisker to Make Plug-in Hybrids at Former GM Plant." *New York Times*, October 26, 2009. www.nytimes.com.

Eder, Andrew. "Chrysler Slamming Its Doors Shut Early." *News Journal*, October 24, 2008.

Milford, Maureen. "2,100 Autoworkers to Lose Jobs by 2009." *News Journal*, February 15, 2007.

Morning News. "Chrysler to Build Huge Tank Arsenal near Newark Plant." December 23, 1951.

News Journal. "For Seven Decades, the Auto Assembly Site Was a Landmark in Newark." October 24, 2008.

———. "Newark Plant Highlights." January 30, 2001.

Simmons, Karie. "Former Chrysler Workers Remember the Site's Past, Celebrate Its Future." *Newark Post*, November 3, 2015. www.newarkpostonline.com.

Boxwood Road

Baker, Karl. "Demolition of Shuttered Boxwood GM Plant Brings Hope of New Delaware Jobs." *News Journal*, November 30, 2018.

Cherry, Amy. "Boxwood Bustling Again as a New, Massive Amazon Fulfillment Center Opens Its Doors." WDEL. September 21, 2021. www.wdel.com.

DelawareOnline/*News Journal*, November 30, 2018. www.delawareonline.com.

Eichmann, Mark. "Hopes for Rebirth at Former Delaware Auto Plant." WHYY. July 5, 2018. https://whyy.org.

Holveck, Brandon. "Delaware Losing Bragging Rights for Biggest Amazon Warehouse. Who's Claiming the Title?" DelawareOnline/*The News Journal*, August 1, 2022. www.delawareonline.com.

Journal-Every Evening. "General Motors to Build Plant Here." May 19, 1945.

Lyne, Jack. "Driving Home for Thanksgiving." *Site Selection*. November 23, 2009. https://siteselection.com.

National Public Radio. "GM Ex-Worker On Closing of Delaware Plant." June 1, 2009. www.npr.org.

Rouse, Whitni, and Vince Lattanzio. "General Motors Shutting the Engine on Delaware Plant." NBC 10 Philadelphia. June 1, 2009. www.nbcphiladelphia.com.

Strohl, Daniel. "Wrecking Ball Swings for Former GM Plant in Wilmington, Delaware." *Hemmings*. December 5, 2018. www.hemmings.com.

Lewes's Menhaden Fishery

German, Myna. "The Menhaden Fish—A Staple of Lewes' Colonial Economy." Delaware Public Media. June 24, 2016. www.delawarepublic.org.

MacArthur, Ron. "Menhaden Fleet Provides Flashback in Lewes History." *Cape Gazette*, September 23, 2022. www.capegazette.com.

Murray, Molly. "When Menhaden Fishing Was a Way of Life in Lewes; Del. Town Was a Center of Industry." *Baltimore Sun*, September 29, 1993. www.baltimoresun.com.

Building Ships

Delaware Public Media. "History Matters: Shipbuilding Industry along the Wilmington Riverfront." July 22, 2016. www.delawarepublic.org.

———. "History Matters: The Origins of Shipbuilding in Sussex County." June 24, 2016. www.delawarepublic.org.

Hutchinson, Henry H. "Collected Notes on Bethel, (formerly Lewisville) Del." *The Archeolog*, March 1969, www.delawarearchaeology.org.

MacArthur, Ron. "Shipbuilding in Sussex Was Really Big Business." *Cape Gazette*, June 17, 2022. www.capegazette.com.

Milford Museum. "Milford Shipyards." www.milforddemuseum.org.

Hartmann & Fehrenbach Brewing Company

Medkeff, John. "Hartmann & Fehrenbach." Delaware Beer History. www.delawarebeerhistory.com.

Stevenson, Judy. "Hartmann & Fehrenbach Brewing Company." Hagley Museum and Library. October 31, 2021. www.hagley.org.

Sussex Stills

Morgan, Michael. *Delaware Prohibition*. Charleston, SC: The History Press, 2021.

War Machine on the Brandywine

Baldwin Brown, Nona. "The Vestiges of a Life That Gunpowder Built." *New York Times*, April 11, 1976. www.nytimes.com.

Delaware Herald. "The Gun-Powder Explosion." June 14, 1854.

Hagley Museum. "The DuPont Company on the Brandywine: Company Chronology: 1801–1834." www.hagley.org.

Rensberger, Boyce. "Explore DuPont's Gunpowder Mills on the Brandywine." *Washington Post*, May 14, 1997. www.washingtonpost.com.

Spring Pfeifer, Hannah. "Du Pont: From French Exiles to the Toast of the Brandywine." *Inside Adams*, Library of Congress Blogs, July 26, 2021. https://blogs.loc.gov.

Shell House

Bies, Jessica. "Delaware's Most Expensive House on Market: Rehoboth Beach Home Has Ties to Wealth, History." *News Journal*, April 15, 2019.

Flood, Chris. "Century-old Shell House Comes Down." *Cape Gazette*, August 4, 2020.

Forney, Dennis. "Between Ocean and Lake, Delaware's Most Expensive Residence." *Cape Gazette*, March 1, 2019.

Jacobs, Fay. "A Wild Part of Our Gay History Is Gone." *CAMP Rehoboth*, August 14, 2020.

Lawrence

Maynard, W. Barksdale. "Lawrence." SAH Archipedia, https://sah-archipedia.org.

Morning News. "Seaford Civic Leader Dallas D. Culver Dies." October 2, 1978.

National Park Service. "Lawrence." National Register of Historic Places Inventory Nomination Form. November 18, 1977. https://npgallery.nps.gov.

Shortridge, Dan. "Sussex Preservationists Working to Save—Or at Least Document—Historic Houses." *News Journal*, March 24, 2008.

Ghosts of Cannon Hall

Journal-Every Evening. "Blighted Romance and Tragedy Figure in Ferry Founders Era." May 2, 1952.

Lynch, Nancy E. "Couple Rebuilds Historic Cannon Hall." *News Journal*, July 14, 2014. www.delawareonline.com.

Maynard, W. Barksdale. "Cannon Hall." SAH Archipedia. https://sah-archipedia.org.

National Park Service. "Cannon's (Woodland) Ferry." National Register of Historic Places Inventory Nomination Form. July 10, 1972. https://npgallery.nps.gov.

Parks, Lynn. "'Ghost' Strolls Woodland's Cannon Hall." *News Journal*, September 9, 1998.

Sanginiti, Terri. "Cause of Historic Mansion's Demise Under Investigation." *News Journal*, October 20, 2010.

Silva, Annette. "This Old House Has Tales to Tell." *News Journal*, September 15, 1993.

Stump, Brice. "Woodland's Historic Landmark Set to Make a Big Comeback." *Daily Times*, August 5, 2014. www.delmarvanow.com.

Woodlawn

Fowser, Mark. "'Greek Tragedy': Stately Smyrna Restaurant / Farmhouse Demolished for Development." WDEL. July 21, 2017. www.wdel.com.

Gronau, Ian. "Historic Thomas England House Demolished." *Delaware State News*, July 14, 2017. https://baytobaynews.com.

Maynard, W. Barksdale. "Thomas England House Restaurant (Woodlawn)." SAH Archipedia. https://sah-archipedia.org.

National Park Service. "Woodlawn / The Thomas England House." National Register of Historic Places Inventory Nomination Form. September 16, 1982. https://catalog.archives.gov/id/75323979.

The Hermitage

Evening Journal. "Historic 'Hermitage' House In New Castle Hit by Fire." April 1, 1970.

Journal-Every Evening. "New Castle Restoration Plans Given Boost in Hermitage Sale." June 29, 1949.
National Park Service. "The Hermitage." National Register of Historic Places Inventory Nomination Form. March 1, 1973. https://npgallery.nps.gov.
Sanginiti, Terri. "The Hermitage Blaze Ruled Arson by State Fire Marshal." *News Journal*, April 13, 2007.

Tilton General Hospital

Armed Center of History and Heritage. "James Tilton." https://achh.army.mil.
Dixon, Mark E. "How an 18th-Century Doctor from Dover Was Ahead of His Time." *Delaware Today*, April 13, 2017. https://delawaretoday.com.
Howell, Jordan. "In Wilmington, Tilton Park Betrays Inequity of Urban Green Spaces." WHYY. October 15, 2015. https://whyy.org.
Ryan, Tom. "Civil War Profiles: Tilton General Hospital, a Haven for Civil War Casualties." *Coastal Point*, August 14, 2013. www.coastalpoint.com.

A City of Three Hospitals

ChristianaCare. "Who We Are: Our History." https://christianacare.org.
Delaware Today. "Homeopathic Care Before It Was Trendy." July 14, 2014. https://delawaretoday.com.

Emily Bissell Hospital

American Experience. "TB in America: 1895–1954." www.pbs.org.
Centers for Disease Control and Prevention. "TB 101 for Health Care Workers." www.cdc.gov.
Hughes, Isabel. "Life & Death: A Ghost Hunters Dream." *News Journal*, July 24, 2022.
Mill Creek Hundred History Blog. "Emily P. Bissell." July 9, 2010. http://mchhistory.blogspot.com.
News Journal. "Name Change to Be Asked." January 25, 1957.
Rini, Jen. "Emily Bissell Hospital to Close." *News Journal*, September 23, 2015.

The Nanticoke Language

Clark, Charles C. IV. "The Nanticoke Story." *Delaware Beach Life*, September 2017.

Jackson, Rachael. "Nanticoke Try to Bring Ancient Tongue to Life." *News Journal*, March 17, 2007.

Journal Every-Evening. "Rediscovery of Lydia Clark's Grave Tends to Substantiate Legends of Delaware Indians." December 24, 1935.

Lynch Steele, Nancy. "The Witness: Lydia Clark's Testimony in a Racially Charged 1855 Case Impacted Sussex County's Native Americans for Generations." *News Journal*, March 6, 2016.

Morning News. "Unveil Memorial to Indian Woman." November 14, 1927.

Short, Michael. "Nanticoke Tribe Seeks to Revive Its Lost Language." andrewsharp.net (formerly the *Delaware Independent*). www.andrewsharp.net.

Cheney Clow's Fort

Federal Writers' Project. *Delaware: A Guide to the First State*. Edited by Jeannette Eckman, Anthony Higgins and William H. Conner. New York: Viking Press, 1938.

Hoffecker, Carol E. *Delaware: A Bicentennial History*. New York: W.W. Norton & Company, 1977.

Miller, J.L. "A Revolutionary Legend Is Born." *News Journal*, July 4, 1997.

National Park Service. "Scene of Cheney Clow's Rebellion." January 4, 1973, https://npgallery.nps.gov.

Delaware's POW Camps

Brown, Jeff. "German Prisoners of War a Common Sight in Delaware during Waning Years of World War II." *News Journal*, May 29, 2017. www.delawareonline.com.

MacArthur, Ron. "Sussex County's Little-Known Connections to World War II." *Cape Gazette*, June 3, 2022._www.capegazette.com.

Roysdon, Keith. "German POW Camps in the U.S. Co-Existed with Their Towns in Sometimes Odd Ways." *Daily Yonder*, March 10, 2022. https://dailyyonder.com.

The Prison at Prices Corner

Talorico, Patricia, and Esteban Parra. "Delaware to Demolish a 1929 Prices Corner Prison That Historians Say Is 'One of a Kind.'" *News Journal*, September 27, 2022. www.delawareonline.com.

The Whipping Post

Baltazar, Rony. Personal communication, August 10, 2023.
Cherry, Amy. " 'An Insult…Every Time I Rode By': State's Last Whipping Post to Be Removed in Georgetown." WDEL. June 30, 2020. www.wdel.com.
Delaware Division of Historic and Cultural Affairs. "Whipping Post to Be Removed from Public Display." June 30, 2020. https://news.delaware.gov.
Dixon, Mark E. "Unpacking the History of Delaware's Whipping Post." *Delaware Today*. June 7, 2017. https://delawaretoday.com.
Frank, William P. "Whipping Post's Exit Recalls Dark History." *Evening Journal*, July 11, 1972.
Lauria, Maddy, and Xerxes Wilson. "Delaware Residents Celebrate Departure of Local Whipping Post from Public Land." *News Journal*, July 1, 2020. www.delawareonline.com.

Glenville

Miller, Beth. "First of Flood-Prone Glenville Homes Demolished." *News Journal*, August 20, 2005.
———. "Flash Floods Soak Region as Isabel Heads for Coast." *News Journal*, September 16, 2003.
———. "In Glenville, Family Holds On to Dream Home." *News Journal*, December 26, 2005.
———. "In Glenville, It's Time to Say Goodbye." *News Journal*, August 16, 2005.

Laurel's Lewis Mural

Parra, Esteban. "Laurel Mural Spared Demolition." *News Journal*, April 4, 1997.
Rivera, Patricia. "Laurel Building and Mural May Be Saved." *News Journal*, May 2, 1997.
———. "Laurel Puts Landmarks on Display." *News Journal*, August 2, 1993.
Roth, Nick. "Revered Artist Jack Lewis's Life, Works Remembered." *Cape Gazette*, August 24, 2012. www.capegazette.com.
WHYY. "Delaware Artist Jack Lewis Dies." August 21, 2012. https://whyy.org.

Friendship Fire

Scharf, John. *History of Delaware: 1609–1888*. Philadelphia: L.J. Richards & Co., 1888.
University of Delaware Library. "Records of the Friendship Fire Company of Wilmington, Delaware." https://library.udel.edu.

Little Creek Friends Meeting

Anderson, Craig. "Area Quakers Rejoice Over New Cemetery Wall." *Delaware State News*, November 19, 2015. https://baytobaynews.com.
Work Projects Administration. "Inventory of the Church Archives of Delaware by the Historical Records Survey." March 1940. https://archivesfiles.delaware.gov.

The Church of Jesus Christ of Latter-day Saints

Church of Jesus Christ of Latter-day Saints. "Facts and Statistics: Delaware." https://newsroom.churchofjesuschrist.org.
Evening Journal. "To Give Mormon Lectures in Park." August 15, 1922.
Every Evening. "Church of Jesus Christ." May 28, 1927.
——. "To Discuss Mormonism." September 11, 1920.
Journal-Every Evening. "Mormons Hear Visiting Elder." October 30, 1937.
Morning News. "Latter-Day Saints." January 16, 1926.
———. "Mormon." June 26, 1937.

Work Projects Administration. "Inventory of the Church Archives of Delaware by the Historical Records Survey." March 1940. https://archivesfiles.delaware.gov.

Christ UMC

Black Dog Salvage. "Season 8 Episode 1: Former United Methodist Church." September 17, 2017. https://blackdogsalvage.com.
Christ United Methodist Church. "About Us." February 29, 2016. https://web.archive.org.
Delaware Public Archives. "Christ United Methodist Church." https://archives.delaware.gov.
Walker, Derby. "What's Happening with the Church Tower Wall?" *Good News from Christ Church*, March 2016. https://web.archive.org.
Zebley, Frank. *The Churches of Delaware.* Wilmington, DE: Frank R. Zebley, 1947.

Chesed Shel Emeth

Journal-Every Evening. "600 March With Scrolls." January 6, 1958.
"Over 100 Years of Active Jewish Life in Delaware." *Shalom Delaware*, July 2018. www.shalomdelaware.org.
Wagman, Mark. "Adas Kodesch Shel Emeth: Over 125 Years of Family and Tradition." Adas Kodesch Shel Emeth. akse.org.
Works Progress Administration. "Inventory of the Church Archives of Delaware by the Historical Records Survey." March 1940. https://archivesfiles.delaware.gov.
Zebley, Frank. *The Churches of Delaware.* Wilmington, DE: Frank R. Zebley, 1947.

Forwood School

Nagengast, Larry. "Examining Plans for the Former Forwood School Site." Delaware Public Media. July 28, 2023. www.delawarepublic.org.
———. "Final Act in Forwood School's Demise Nears." Delaware Public Media. April 13, 2018. www.delawarepublic.org.

Slaughter Neck School

Skelcher, Bradley. *African American Education in Delaware: A History Through Photographs, 1865–1940*. Dover, DE: Delaware Heritage Press, 2007.

Ross Point School

Kipp, Rachel, and Dan Shortridge. *Secret Delaware.* St. Louis, MO: Reedy Press, 2022.

National Park Service. "National Register of Historic Places Registration Form—Ross Point School." July 12, 2001. https://npgallery.nps.gov.

The Inlet Bridge

Diehl, James. *Remembering Sussex County: From Zwaanendael to King Chicken*. Charleston, SC: The History Press, 2009.

MacArthur, Ron. "Inlet Bridge History Dates Back Nearly Nine Decades." *Cape Gazette*, January 27, 2023. www.capegazette.com.

Vanished Railroads

Cape Gazette. "Blue Diamond Railroad Lasts Only Six Months." February 7, 2023. www.capegazette.com.

Poore, Douglas. *Abandoned Railroads of Delmarva.* Charleston, SC: Arcadia Publishing, 2021.

Queen Anne Pier

Cape Gazette. "Milton-Ellendale Segment of Queen Anne's Railroad Still Functional." May 21, 2019. www.capegazette.com.

Journal-Every Evening. "Part of Pier Destroyed." September 19, 1936.

Morning News. "Broken Pier Drifts as Lewes Ice Melts." February 27, 1936.

———. "Owner to Restore Old Pier at Lewes." May 15, 1936.

Murray, Molly. "Book Recounts Pier, Maritime Exchange." *News Journal*, July 5, 1989.

Smith's Bridge and Wooddale Bridge

Atlas Obscura. "Ashland Bridge." www.atlasobscura.com.
———. "Wooddale Bridge." www.atlasobscura.com.
Barksdale, W. Maynard. "Smith"s Bridge." SAH Archipedia. https://sah-archipedia.org.
The Brandywine. "Smith Bridge, Chadds Ford, PA." www.thebrandywine.com.
Evening Journal. "Fire Wrecks Smith Bridge While Vandals Prowl Area." October 31, 1961.
———. "Smith's Bridge Restoration Voted; Cost Put at $75,000." November 9, 1961.
O'Sullivan, Sean. "149 Glenville Homes Declared Uninhabitable." *News Journal*, September 17, 2003.

The Delaplane

Evening Journal. "Airship Taken to Hare's Corner." July 12, 1911.
———. "Bloomfield Goes Up in Delaplane." July 3, 1911.
———. "Delaplane Flies Some." October 22, 1910.
———. "No Flying yet in Delaplane." July 17, 1911.
———. "Wilmington Aero Club's 'Delaplane,' a Biplane Built for the Club by Robie Seidlinger, the Inventor." October 5, 1910.
Every Evening. "The Aero Club's Machine Tested." November 21, 1910.
———. "'Delaplane' Described." October 26, 1910.
———. "No Flight Attempted." October 25, 1910.
Frebert, George J. *Delaware Aviation History*. Dover, DE: Dover Litho Printing Company, 1998.
Morning News. "Aero Club Plans to Assist Fair with Aviation Meet." July 29, 1911.
———. "Aeroplane Model." November 14, 1910.
———. "Aviator Makes Three Flights in Delaplane." July 3, 1911.
———. "Delaplane Sails on Its First Test." October 22, 1910.

Bellanca Airfield

Frebert, George J. *Delaware Aviation History*. Dover, DE: Dover Litho Printing, 1998.

Herald News (Passaic, NJ). "Giuseppe Bellanca, Airplane Builder, Once Area Resident." December 27, 1960.

Larson, George C. "Making a Smoother (and Speedier) Airplane." *Air & Space Magazine*, July 2012. www.smithsonianmag.com.

Maryland Historical Trust. "K-155: Shorewood (Wilson Point, Wilmer Point)." January 23, 2020. https://mht.maryland.gov.

Morning News. "Developer Buys Bellanca Field." December 8, 1960.

———. "G.M. Bellanca, Local Aviation Pioneer, Dies." December 27, 1960.

———. "36 'Drag' Fans Pay Up; Bellanca Brakes Stay." April 26, 1962.

Port Mahon Light

Caddell, Ted. "Last Light Blazes at Landmark Lighthouse." *News Journal*, December 30, 1984.

Dallabrida, Dale A. "Memories Still Shine: Port Mahon Lighthouse Was Focus of the Bay's Vibrant History."

Delaware Gazette and State Journal. "For Lights on the Delaware." February 21, 1895.

Journal Every-Evening. "Mrs. Janie E. Lynch." April 5, 1954.

Morning News. February 14, 1985.

Smyrna Times. "Lighthouse Went Cheap." July 29, 1903.

———. "Sale of Light House Paraphernalia." July 15, 1903.

Cape Henlopen Light

Morning News. "Henlopen Ruins Lure Collectors." April 15, 1926.

———. "Many Calls after Henlopen Crash." May 5, 1926.

News Journal. "Henlopen Light Wreckage Sought by Relic Hunters." April 14, 1926.

Roth, Nick. "Cape Henlopen Lighthouse Still Stands Tall in Cape Region History." *Cape Gazette*, April 13, 2016.

Trapiani, Bob, Jr. *Delaware Lights: A History of Lighthouses in the First State.* Charleston, SC: The History Press, 2007.

INDEX

C

D

L

M

N

Z

ABOUT THE AUTHORS

Rachel Kipp and Dan Shortridge are a husband-and-wife writing duo who have penned several other books about Delaware. Former newspaper journalists, they enjoy exploring the hidden stories of the First State and surrounding areas and sharing them with their readers. Rachel has worked in communications, marketing and content for the University of Pennsylvania and the Philadelphia Bar Association. Dan has led communications and public relations and developed content for several Delaware state agencies and a regional marketing firm. The parents of three, they enjoy traveling, finding new eateries, hiking and the outdoors.